# BOY SCOUTS OF AMERICA
## MERIT BADGE SERIES

# PAINTING

*"Enhancing our youths' competitive edge through merit badges"*

BOY SCOUTS OF AMERICA®

35926
ISBN 978-0-8395-3372-6
©2016 Boy Scouts of America
2019 Printing

# Requirements

1. Explain the proper safety procedures to follow when preparing surfaces and applying coatings.

2. Do the following:

    a. Explain three ways that coatings can improve a surface.

    b. Explain the differences between oil-based paints, acrylic-based paints, and water-based paints.

    c. Explain where you would apply enamel paint, flat paint, wood stain, and varnish, and explain the importance of sheen.

    d. Tell why each is best for these uses.

3. Prepare and paint two different surfaces using patching material, caulking, and the proper primers and topcoats. Suggested projects include an interior or exterior wall, a door, a piece of furniture, a concrete wall or floor, a porch rail, or a fence. Your counselor must preapprove the projects.

4. Prepare and paint an item using harmonizing colors that you have selected using the color wheel in this book.

5. Show the right way to use, clean, maintain, and store painting equipment.

6. Explain the importance of ladder safety, environmental responsibility, and personal hygiene when painting.

7. Explain some of the environmental and health issues concerning removing paint, applying paint, and discarding old paint.

8. Find out about career opportunities in the paint industry. Discuss the training and experience required, and explain why this profession might interest you.

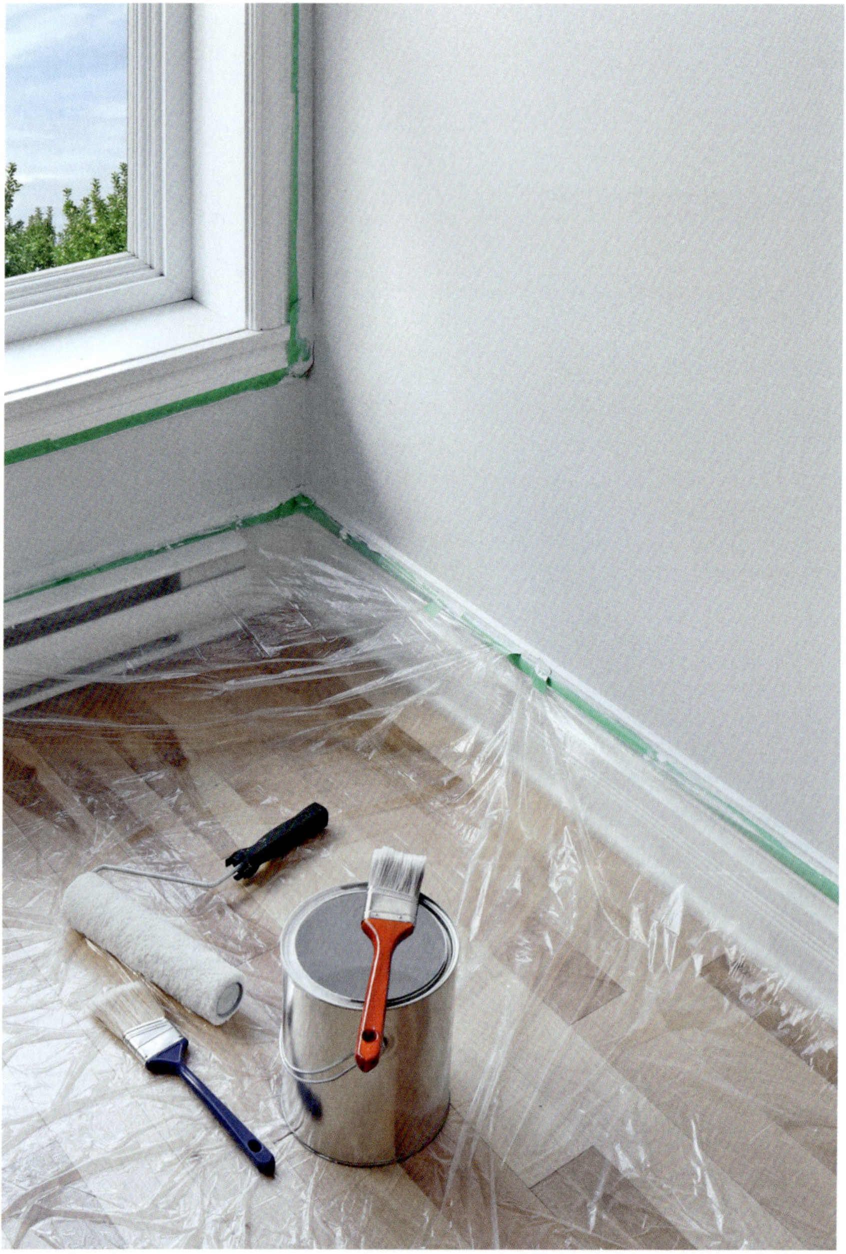

## Contents

Introduction . . . . . . . . . . . . . . . . . . . . . . . . . . . . . . . . . . . . . 7

Safety and Environmental Responsibility . . . . . . . . . . . . . . 13

Color . . . . . . . . . . . . . . . . . . . . . . . . . . . . . . . . . . . . . . . . . 29

All About Paint . . . . . . . . . . . . . . . . . . . . . . . . . . . . . . . . . 39

Surface Preparation . . . . . . . . . . . . . . . . . . . . . . . . . . . . . 45

Application Equipment and Procedures . . . . . . . . . . . . . . . 53

Opportunities in the Painting Craft . . . . . . . . . . . . . . . . . . . 67

Glossary . . . . . . . . . . . . . . . . . . . . . . . . . . . . . . . . . . . . . . 71

Painting Resources . . . . . . . . . . . . . . . . . . . . . . . . . . . . . . 77

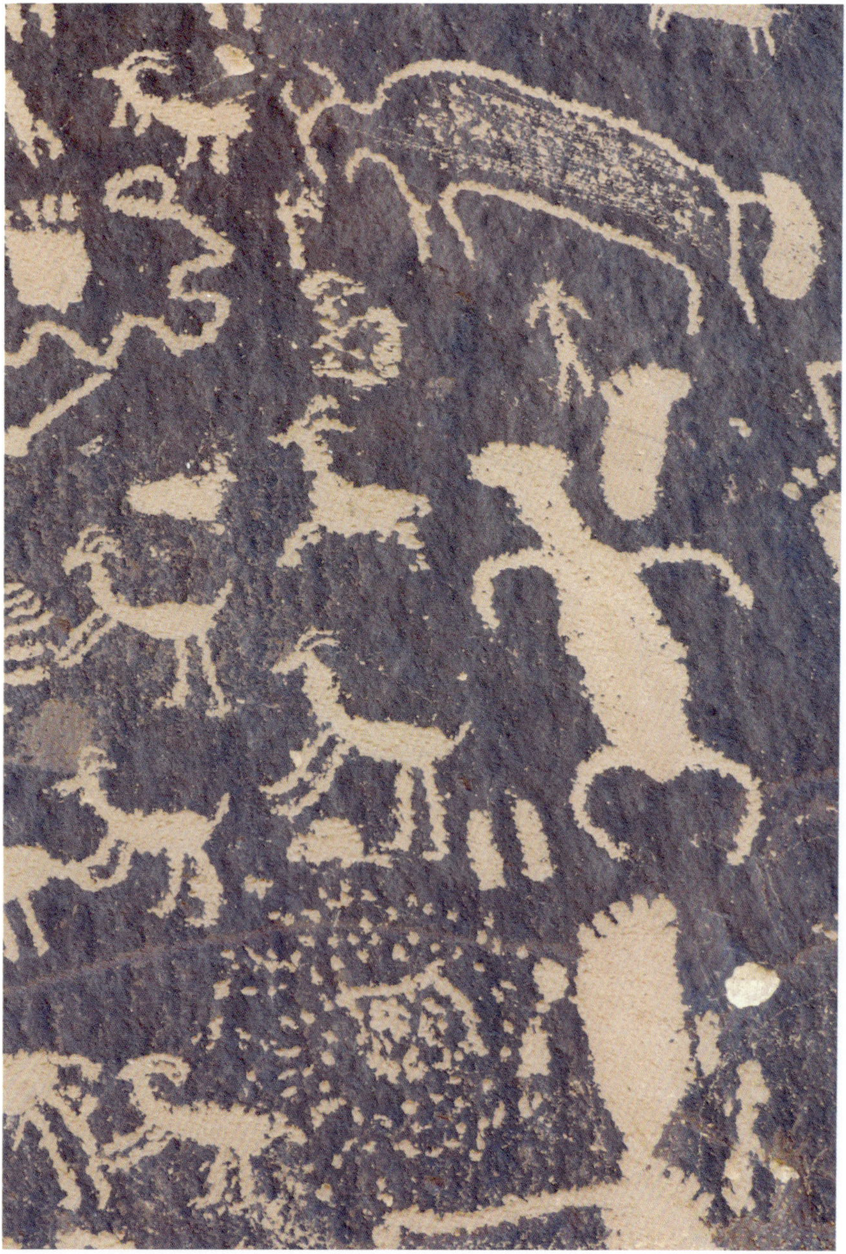

# Introduction

Human beings everywhere have always decorated their shelter, no matter how crude or humble that dwelling was. Some scientists believe that murals in caves in Altamira, Spain, and Lascaux Grotto, France, date to 30,000 B.C. Prehistoric painters were limited to colors made from *pigments* found in natural materials such as minerals. For example, the pigment called ochre—from iron ore—made paints that were yellow, red, brown, and black.

Although the Egyptians are credited with the discovery of *varnish,* the Asian cultures were among the first to develop paints, using pigmented—colored—crayons with clay as a *binder.* The use of *lacquers* and varnishes in China dates back to prehistoric times.

While protective painting was not done in Europe until the 12th century, Egyptians, Greeks, Romans, Asians, and Incas were painting buildings as early as the second century B.C. The Greeks and Romans added a greater range of colors to their paints and varnishes and began applying paints to house exteriors, ships, sculptures, decorations, and wall paintings. Although the Romans first introduced paints into Europe, European artists in search of new colors and more versatile types of paints were largely responsible for the evolution of paint up to the 17th century.

In Colonial America, the oil-based paints that were available were difficult to level and required as many as nine coats. These layers of paint were topped with a hard, glossy coat, which produced a rich finish. "Rich" is the key word because this process was very expensive. As a result, the home of the average colonial was not painted at all. However, such a complicated treatment made for a finish that would last for decades.

Terms shown in *italics* can be found in the glossary at the back of this pamphlet.

**PAINTING** 7

# Introduction

> Have you ever noticed that you do not see many 250-year-old cottages or cabins? Very few, if any, buildings owned by people who didn't have money for paint are still standing. Because they were left unprotected from the elements, most of those houses have not survived.

As a less expensive alternative to paint, many people used whitewash, made from quicklime (calcium oxide) mixed with water.

The result of this wealth can be seen in early American houses today throughout New England and the original Colonies. These dwellings were homes of wealthy Americans. The fact that, more than 200 years later, many of these homes have remained standing has a lot to do with those nine coats of paint.

After the mid-1700s, "barn red" became a popular and widely used paint color because of its warmth and low-cost iron-oxide pigment. Other popular colors were pumpkin, yellow, cream, and white. Paint also was used for interior woodwork to complement expensive imported wallpaper that the average citizen could not afford.

After 1875, factory-made paints were available at a reasonable cost. As a result, greater numbers of people painted and decorated more of their buildings, and more frequently.

# Recent Developments

Since the end of the 19th century, technology has changed the craft of painting. Advances have been made in paint materials, surface preparation, paint application, and quality control. Increased attention to environmental and safety regulations has hastened these improvements.

During the 19th and 20th centuries, extensive research efforts uncovered new materials for use in pigments, binders, and *solvents*. Some of these materials are *organic*, which means they originated from a plant or animal. Some are *inorganic*, which means they originated from a mineral. Some are synthetic, or made by humans. Since World War II, new *resins* have improved general-purpose paints and have allowed manufacturers to tailor coatings to specific materials, purposes, and environmental conditions.

In the 20th century, the most significant change was the development of water-based *latex* and *acrylic* paints, which replaced many oil-based coverings. *Alkyd* paints were developed in the 1920s. These paints are made of a synthetic resin—alkyd—that is derived from a specific kind of acid in reaction with a specific kind of alcohol. The properties of alkyds are similar to oils, and the two materials can be mixed. Alkyd-modified resins, however, dry faster than natural oils.

Despite these advances in technology, the need for craftsmanship remains. The craftsperson must choose appropriate colors and tools and apply the paint effectively. Technology will never replace art and old-fashioned craftsmanship.

# Reasons for Painting

There are two basic reasons to paint a surface: to protect it or to decorate it. Often, a painter wants to do both. For projects with certain requirements, a special-purpose paint may be necessary. For example, paint used on a boat bottom contains specific agents to fight the growth of organisms on the hull.

## Introduction

### Protection From Natural Elements

Most outside surfaces break down when exposed to nature's elements—sun, heat, rain, ice, cold, wind, snow. Paint adheres to the surfaces and helps protect them from brutal effects—particularly damage from moisture, which makes wood swell, warp, and rot, and metals rust and corrode. The more vulnerable interior wall surfaces, such as drywall and plaster, also can be damaged when exterior surfaces have been neglected.

### Decoration for Living Areas

Paint has always been used primarily for decoration. The need to make our surroundings more attractive and uplifting is usually the main reason we decide to paint. Whether you are painting your home or Fido's home, part of the satisfaction you get from the finished job is its pleasant appearance.

**This fine example of a mural can be found at Sundance Square in downtown Fort Worth, Texas.**

### How Paint Can Improve a Surface

New technology and materials used in paint today increase the ways paint and other coatings can improve a surface. From water-based acrylics to oil-based alkyds, the choices available offer a variety of benefits.

Paint can improve the appearance of an old structure, protect the surface from harmful elements, and help prevent it from aging further. Paints made for marine or swimming pool use can even make vessels and pools resistant to organisms and harsh chemicals. Many paints, such as automobile paints, are specially designed to provide a hard, protective barrier against the environment and the hundreds of washings a car must withstand. Paints designed with special reflective properties are used to stripe roads and make highways safer.

Lastly, paint improves a surface and enhances the entire structure, which increases its financial value.

## Painting for Special Effects

*Faux* (pronounced "foe," and meaning false) finishes play tricks on your eyes and can make a surface look as if it is made of marble, parchment, or leather, for instance. Wood can be painted to look like stone, and metal can look like wood. Faux finishing is used to make smaller rooms look larger and flat surfaces appear three-dimensional.

Special painting techniques, including glazing, marbling, graining, antiquing, stippling, texturing, and gilding can be used to make an otherwise plain room or piece of furniture appear fancy. Trompe l'oeil (pronounced "tromp loy"), meaning "trick the eye," is a way of painting a surface to give the illusion that something is real—like a sky on a ceiling.

Another special painting technique is *stenciling*. Even a person with no artistic talent can paint virtually any design with a stencil pattern. The painter uses a stencil brush to paint the design through the perforated pattern.

A decorative paint job sometimes has surprising effects. For example, one rarely sees graffiti on an urban mural brightening a parking lot.

**The Forum Shops at Caesars, in Las Vegas, Nevada, uses trompe l'oeil throughout to create special effects.**

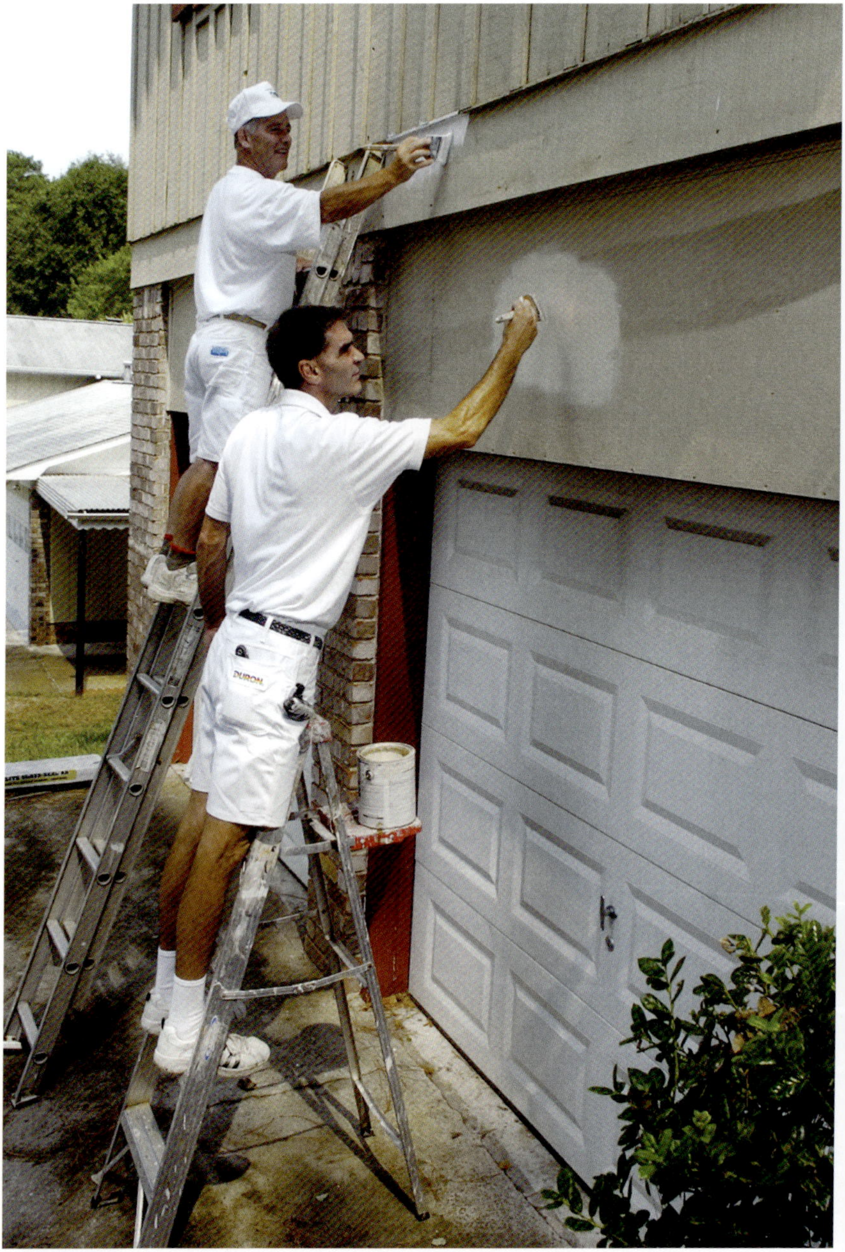

# Safety and Environmental Responsibility

Using painting products and equipment requires some basic knowledge to stay safe and help protect the environment.

## Putting Safety First

Using painting materials and tools carries a degree of risk. Ingredients in paint can cause simple allergic reactions or chronic, long-term ill health effects. Misusing hand and power tools and ladders can cause injuries ranging from minor to life-threatening.

Setting up a painting project also can involve risk. The most important tool for improving safety is attitude. Promote an attitude of safety as you learn about painting and earn the Painting merit badge, and the fun will follow.

## Planning and Training

Planning a painting job is critical to safety. Accidents usually can be prevented with proper planning. Anticipate dangers and plan ways to avoid them. Learning how to use tools and materials properly is important. Make sure to read and understand proper operating instructions before using any equipment. Read the label and manual.

> Be committed to safety by keeping informed about safe practices. Review tasks before beginning them, and maintain high standards of safety.

## Safety and Environmental Responsibility

### Alertness

It is easy to be distracted when you are tired or bored. To keep safe while painting, stay alert to what is going on so you can recognize dangers and take steps to eliminate or avoid them.

If you must listen to the radio or music while you work, keep the volume low. Accidents can occur when music is playing too loudly because you aren't paying enough attention to your work environment.

### Personal Protective Equipment

The best way to keep safe from toxins is to make sure the materials are completely toxin-free. Many paint materials do contain toxic chemicals, however, so take other measures to control the environment.

The main factor you control in any task is yourself. Whether preparing the surface for painting or applying paint, wear the appropriate personal protective equipment. Remember, previously applied paint might also contain dangerous contaminants from which you should protect yourself.

> Let the professionals do the dirty work. Never attempt to remove lead-based paint. Only qualified professional painting contractors should take on this dangerous task. The Environmental Protection Agency outlines requirements that contractors must follow. See the resources section for more information.

**Appropriate Clothing.** Many professional painters wear suits specially designed to protect them from toxic materials. While you may not have or require this kind of suit, you still should wear protective, long-sleeved clothing made of a heavy fabric such as canvas or denim. Protect your feet by wearing heavy work shoes or boots.

**Eye Protection.** It is very easy to get something in your eyes while painting, especially when you are removing paint and preparing surfaces. Wear safety glasses or goggles to keep paint and debris out of your eyes.

**Respirator.** Many paint materials contain chemicals that are dangerous to inhale. And when you remove old paint, dust can sometimes be harmful. To protect yourself, always wear the appropriate *respirator*. Consult the *safety data sheet,* or SDS, which is discussed later in this section.

Respirators range from inexpensive dust masks available at most home improvement or discount stores to sophisticated air-supply hoods. Keep the respirator clean and in good repair.

**Gloves.** When selecting gloves, make certain they offer protection from the chemical to which you will be exposed. The safety data sheet or the label on the paint container should have guidelines about appropriate protective equipment. (See more about the safety data sheet later in this section.)

**Hard Hat.** At times during the project, you may need to wear a hard hat for protection from any falling items or to keep from hitting your head on different surfaces.

## Personal Hygiene

While working, painters constantly have contact with chemicals—in paints, solvents, strippers, or other materials. Washing your skin frequently can reduce exposure to toxins that could cause irritation, and it can prevent accidental ingestion of the toxin. When you are through with a job, shower as soon as possible and launder the dirty clothing. The dust in clothing may make a person ill, so keep the clothing away from people, pets, and clean clothing until you are ready to wash it.

Wash thoroughly before eating or drinking. Never eat or drink in the work area. A painter practicing poor hygiene risks getting contaminants in the mouth or inhaling them.

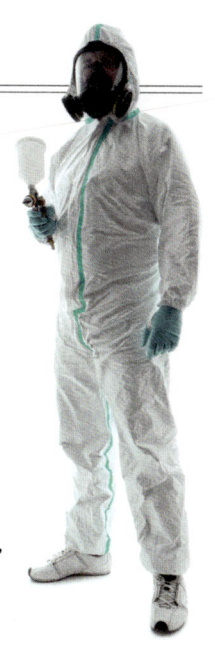

You will get paint and other stains on your clothes, so be sure not to wear street clothing that you don't want to damage.

**PAINTING** 15

SAFETY AND ENVIRONMENTAL RESPONSIBILITY

## Tool Safety

Whether you are using sophisticated power tools or simply a bucket of paint and a brush, you must practice tool safety.

Some tools, called airless sprayers, pump paint at high pressure and may be powered by hazardous fuels. Other tools produce hazards such as noise, dust, and dangerous debris or particles.

### HAND TOOLS

Take care of hand tools and they will last for many years.

=== Safety and Environmental Responsibility

## POWER TOOLS

Take the following precautions when using power tools (such as sanders) to prepare surfaces for paint:

- Follow the manufacturer's instructions for proper and safe operation.

- Guard against injury by using recommended tool guards and wearing protective gear such as goggles and earplugs or earmuffs.

- Use a respirator when dust and vapor hazards are present.

- To avoid shock, make sure that electric tools are adequately grounded; use them only in a dry environment. For added protection, use tools that are double-insulated and are plugged into circuits protected by ground fault circuit interrupters.

- Make sure an abrasive attachment is securely tightened before using a power tool. Disconnect the power before changing or adjusting attachments.

- Run power tools only when they are in contact with the surface to be prepared.

- Inspect equipment regularly, and repair or replace parts on the tool as necessary.

- Do not use power tools in confined spaces where sparks could cause explosions.

### Ladder Safety

Think of safety all the time while using a ladder. Take the time to properly set up the ladder and to use it properly. Taking these precautions can help prevent injury.

The types of ladders most commonly used are the stepladder, which is used to reach just-above-the-head heights, and the extension ladder, which is used for reaching greater heights.

Other types of ladders and climbing equipment include scaffolding, personnel lifts, and suspended work platforms. Professionals use these climbing devices. While it is helpful to know this special equipment exists, you are not required to use any of it to earn the Painting merit badge.

SAFETY AND ENVIRONMENTAL RESPONSIBILITY

**SETUP SAFETY**

- Check ladders for wear, damage, and loose or missing parts.
- Place extension ladders at a safe angle firmly against the wall. For every 4 feet of working height, set the ladder 1 foot away from the base of the structure. If the distance between the bottom and top supports of the ladder is 8 feet, for instance, the ladder should be 2 feet away from the base of the structure, as shown in the illustration.

- Do not set up a ladder in front of a door.
- Make sure that people entering the area can see and avoid the ladder.
- Make sure the ladder is on solid ground; never set a ladder on soft or uneven ground.
- Use caution when working with ladders around electricity. Never use or carry a ladder near power lines or electrical currents.
- On a stepladder, make sure the spreaders between the front and back sections are fully extended and locked into position.
- On an extension ladder, make sure locking devices in the upper section of the ladder securely engage the rungs in the lower section.

8 FEET

2 FEET

18  PAINTING

## CLIMBING SAFETY

- Always face the ladder when climbing or descending, and grasp it firmly.
- Test each rung before putting any weight on it.
- Before climbing, wipe any mud, oil, or wet paint from ladder rungs or steps and from the soles of work shoes. Be sure to wear slip-resistant shoes.
- Never climb higher than the highest standing level marked on a ladder.
- Never rush or skip steps or rungs on a ladder.
- Never allow more than one person on a ladder at a time.
- Never stand or sit on the top, or on the shelf, of a stepladder.

BSA safety guidelines require Scouts to wear a helmet and other safety gear when climbing higher than shoulder height. When a job calls for the painter to climb a ladder higher than shoulder height, it is best left to a professional.

PAINTING 19

# Safety and Environmental Responsibility

## LADDER USE

- Always follow the three-point rule: Keep three parts of your body (two feet and a hand, or two hands and a foot) in contact with the ladder at all times.
- Keep the area around the ladder free from clutter and debris.
- Use ladders as they were intended—don't use a stepladder as a straight ladder, for example.
- Don't use ladders upside down.
- Remove ladders in windy or stormy weather.
- Keep within the ladder's "working load," or weight capacity, including the worker and all equipment. All new ladders have a label stating the weight capacity and other safety information.
- Never leave a ladder unattended, especially around children.
- Keep a safe attitude—never act up or take risks around ladders.

**Whenever using a ladder, follow the three-point rule: Keep three parts of your body (two feet and a hand, or two hands and a foot) in contact with the ladder at all times.**

### Select ladders within the following:

| Type | Duty Rating | Working Load |
|---|---|---|
| IAA | Special duty | 375 lbs. |
| IA | Industrial—extra heavy | 300 lbs. |
| I | Industrial—heavy | 250 lbs. |
| II | Commercial—medium | 225 lbs. |
| III | Household—light | 200 lbs. |

## Materials Safety

Handle painting materials safely. Solvents, paints, paint chips, and dust that may contain lead must be disposed of properly. Paint ingredients, when mishandled, can be dangerous.

**Solvents.** Solvents, such as *mineral spirits,* xylol, and naphtha, are present in some paints and are used to reduce or thin the paint and during cleanup. Solvents are particularly hazardous to the painter and others who may be exposed to them. Follow the same safety guidelines for solvents and solvent-based paints.

Most solvents are toxic when inhaled. Inhaling too many solvent vapors can make breathing difficult, lowering the oxygen level in the body. Always keep the work area well-ventilated by opening all the windows. Keep the air moving by using a fan.

If part of your body comes in contact with a solvent, the result could be harmful. The solvent may leave skin dry and scaly or burn it, leaving it raw and irritated. Wear gloves and keep your hands away from your mouth, eyes, and nose to avoid ingesting solvents or irritating soft body tissues.

**Safe Removal of Paint.** Removing paint is tricky. Once you begin to remove paint, the particles become very small and very easy to ingest by breathing or by talking while your mouth is unprotected. Especially if you are not sure about the origin of the paint that must be removed, it is best to leave this messy and dangerous job to professionals.

All solvent vapors are *flammable*— some are very quick to ignite. Keep solvents away from power equipment, because a single spark from a machine can cause an explosion or fire.

### Is Your House Lead-Free?

*Lead-based paint* can cause serious health problems. Removing it is such a high-risk job that it is best left to a professional. Structures built prior to 1978 are likely to have been painted with lead-based paint. Ask your parents when your house was built. If it was before 1978, or if they are not certain when it was built, do not attempt to use your house as a project. Find something else.

**Never** attempt to remove lead-based paint yourself.

# Safety and Environmental Responsibility

## Fire Safety

The most important point to remember about fire safety is prevention. The best way to prevent fire is to be alert and keep safety in mind when using flammable materials, following the rules described throughout this chapter.

*When you finish a job, clean the equipment thoroughly before storing. Never store rags soaked in paint or solvent. Properly dispose of them in a covered metal waste container.*

**Proper Storage.** It is best to limit the storage of flammable materials. Purchase only the amount needed for a job. If you must store paints and solvents, keep them in a well-ventilated area to avoid buildup of flammable vapors. Never store these materials near a furnace, stove, water heater, or other source of heat. Make sure lids and caps on paint and solvent containers are tightly in place.

Immediately remove clothing that has been soaked with flammable liquid. Keep this clothing separate from other laundry and in a well-ventilated area until you are ready to clean them.

**Fire Extinguishers.** Always keep fire extinguishers near the work area, ready for use at any time.

Just as there is more than one kind of fire, there is more than one kind of fire extinguisher. Multipurpose dry chemical fire extinguishers and carbon dioxide fire extinguishers are the two most common types of fire extinguisher.

Use the class A multipurpose fire extinguisher on ordinary combustible materials such as paper and wood.

For gasoline, grease, paint, and other flammable liquids, use a class B multipurpose or carbon dioxide fire extinguisher.

Live electrical equipment requires the use of a class C multipurpose or carbon dioxide fire extinguisher.

PAINTING

**Ignition Sources.** Any spark can cause a fire around combustible materials. Never use paints or solvents near an open flame or ignition point. Be cautious when using power tools or when working while someone is cutting or welding nearby. Never spray any combustible liquid onto a hot surface.

**Improper Ventilation.** To avoid a dangerous buildup of combustible vapors, always keep the work area well-ventilated.

### Understanding Labels and Safety Data Sheets

To work safely with paint materials, read the *safety data sheet (SDS)* provided by the manufacturer. This document sets forth in great detail how to safely handle the product.

> All paint manufacturers are required by law to provide an SDS so workers will be aware of safety measures to take when working with any particular product.

Make every effort to obtain the SDS for the materials you are using, as you will learn a great deal about the makeup of these materials. Ask a local paint supplier for the SDS on a product. You can also get the SDS for a specific product by contacting the manufacturer (look for a phone number on the product label) or by searching the internet (with your parent's approval).

Paint and solvent cans typically have a lot of detailed information about safe and effective usage and disposal of the product. Although the label on a paint can won't provide the level of detail that an SDS will, read the label carefully, too.

## Safety and Environmental Responsibility

A safety data sheet (SDS) contains 16 sections. While all sections must be included to comply with international regulations, the Occupational Safety and Health Administration will not enforce the content of sections 12 through 15.

Sections 1 through 11 and 16 are described below:

**Section 1: Identification.** This section identifies the chemical on the SDS, lists its recommended uses, and provides the manufacturer's name, address, and emergency telephone contact information.

**Section 2: Hazard(s) Identification.** This section identifies the hazards of the chemical and provides appropriate warning information.

**Section 3: Composition/Information on Ingredients.** This section identifies the ingredients in the product.

**Section 4: First-Aid Measures.** This section describes the initial care that should be given by untrained responders to someone who has been exposed to the chemical.

**Section 5: Fire-Fighting Measures.** This section provides recommendations for fighting a fire caused by the chemical.

**Section 6: Accidental Release Measures.** This section provides recommendations on the appropriate response to spills, leaks, or releases.

**Section 7: Handling and Storage.** This section provides guidance on safe handling and storage practices.

**Section 8: Exposure Controls/Personal Protection.** This section identifies exposure limits and indicates personal protective measures to minimize exposure.

**Section 9: Physical and Chemical Properties.** This section identifies physical and chemical properties associated with the material.

**Section 10: Stability and Reactivity.** This section describes the reactivity hazards of the material and chemical stability information.

**Section 11: Toxicological Information.** This section identifies the toxicological and health effects information or states that such information is not available.

**Section 16: Other Information.** This section includes other information not covered in previous sections, including when the SDS was prepared or last revised.

*Conforms to Regulation (EC) No. 1907/2006 (REACH), Annex II, as amended by Regulation (EU) No. 453/2010*

FIRETEX M71V2
M71V2

# SAFETY DATA SHEET

## SECTION 1: Identification of the substance/mixture and of the company/undertaking

**1.1 Product identifier**

Product name      : FIRETEX M71V2
Product code      : M71V2

**1.2 Relevant identified uses of the substance or mixture and uses advised against**

Material uses     : Paint or paint related material.
                  : Industrial use only.

**1.3 Details of the supplier of the safety data sheet**

Sherwin-Williams Protective & Marine
Tower Works
Kestor Street
Bolton
BL2 2AL
United Kingdom
+44 (0) 1204 521771

---

*Conforms to Regulation (EC) No. 1907/2006 (REACH), Annex II, as amended by Regulation (EU) No. 453/2010*

FIRETEX M71V2
M71V2

## SECTION 2: Hazards identification

Human health hazards     : Irritating to respiratory system. Repeated exposure may cause skin dryness or cracking. Vapours may cause drowsiness and dizziness.

Environmental hazards    : Toxic to aquatic organisms, may cause long-term adverse effects in the aquatic environment.

See Section 16 for the full text of the R phrases or H statements declared above.
See Section 11 for more detailed information on health effects and symptoms.

**2.2 Label elements**

Hazard pictograms   :

Signal word         : Danger
Hazard statements   : Flammable liquid and vapour.
                      May be fatal if swallowed and enters airways.
                      May cause respiratory irritation.
                      May cause drowsiness or dizziness.
                      Toxic to aquatic life with long lasting effects.

**Precautionary statements**

Prevention          : Wear protective gloves. Wear eye or face protection. Keep away from heat, hot surfaces, sparks, open flames and other ignition sources. No smoking. Use explosion-proof electrical, ventilating, lighting and all material-handling equipment. Avoid release to the environment.

Response            : IF INHALED: Remove person to fresh air and keep comfortable for breathing. IF SWALLOWED: Immediately call a POISON CENTER or physician. Do NOT induce vomiting. IF ON SKIN (or hair): Take off immediately all contaminated

## Safety and Environmental Responsibility

Always dispose of any chemical material according to the manufacturer's instructions and local laws.

### Environmental Responsibility

Any activity using chemicals comes with a great risk for polluting the environment, so take great care in all steps of painting and handling materials.

#### Air and Water Pollution

Local, state, and federal regulations apply to hazardous material disposal, so ask your merit badge counselor about regulations that might affect your project. The local Environmental Protection Agency office (look in the government section of the phone book) can tell you more about environmental regulations in your area.

## Safety and Environmental Responsibility

Do not sand or remove old paint that may contain lead, as such efforts may damage the environment and put yourself and others at risk. Particles can disperse into the air or settle on the ground, threatening the health of anyone nearby. Lead contamination can be lethal. Contact a qualified professional painting contractor for projects where lead-based paint may be present.

### Proper Disposal Procedures

Sweep or vacuum any particles of old paint, and properly dispose of this waste. If you do not have enough leftover paint to store, leave the lid off the can and allow the paint to dry out and completely harden before replacing the lid and throwing the can in the trash. This way, the paint will not escape the can and contaminate the environment.

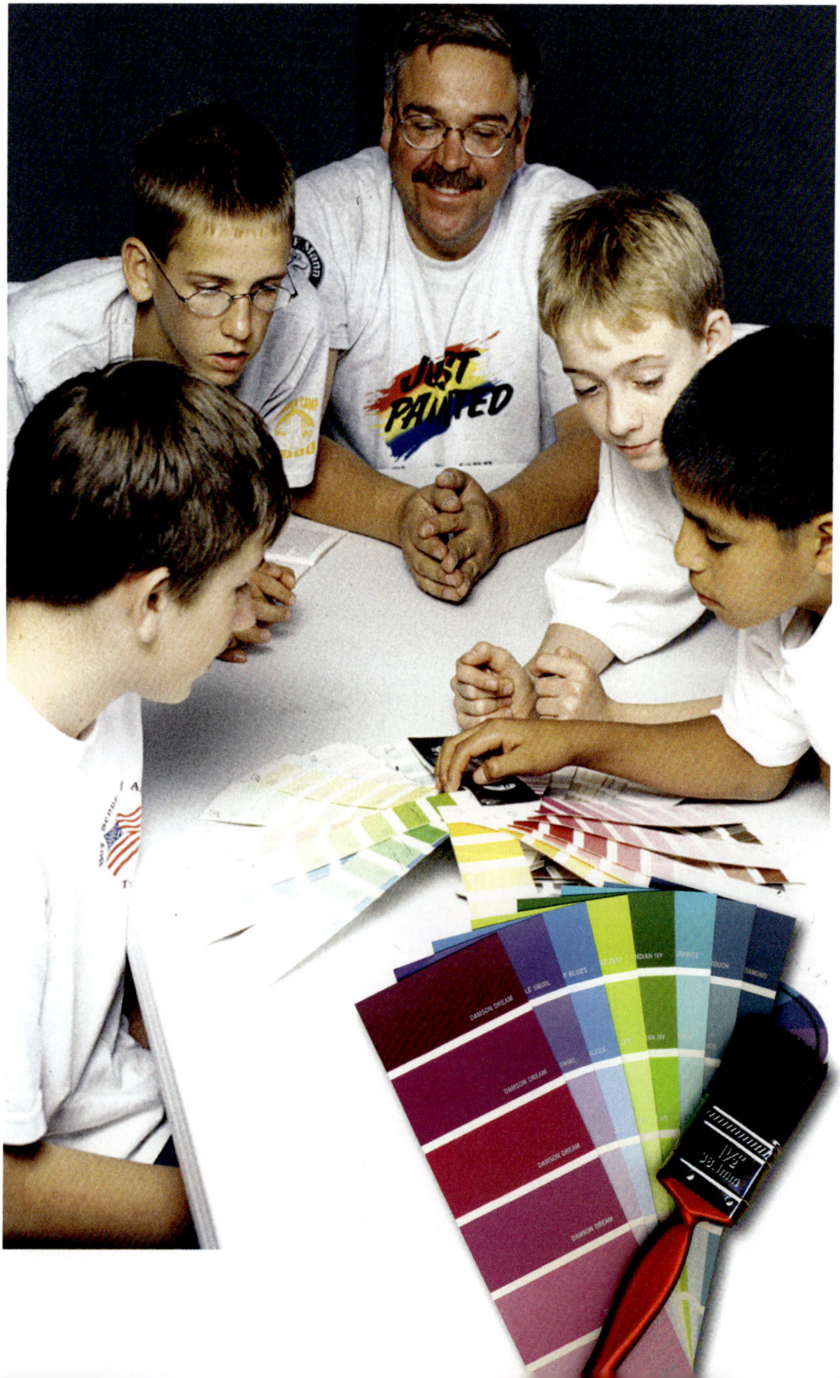
JUST PAINTED
DAMSON DREAM

# Color

Color is the result of three factors: a source of light, an object that has color, and the response of the human eye. The distribution of colors produced when sunlight is dispersed by a prism is known as the *color spectrum*. The color spectrum was discovered by Sir Isaac Newton, the 18th-century English scientist who defined the laws of gravity and motion. Later, scientists in France and Germany discovered they could combine pairs of the *primary* colors—red, yellow, and blue—to create other colors.

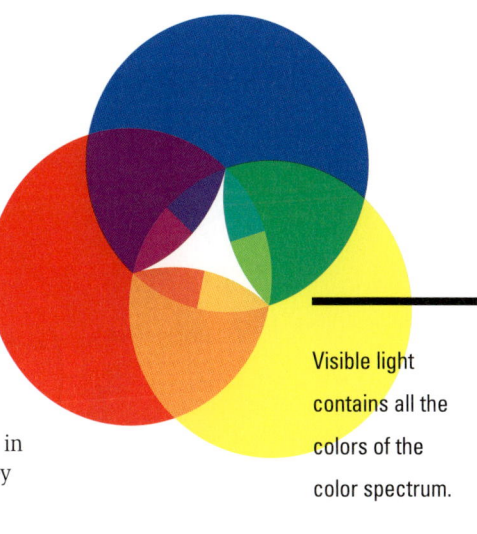

Visible light contains all the colors of the color spectrum.

**Primary color: yellow**   **Secondary color: green**   **Intermediate color: yellow-green**

Our color spectrum today includes the primary colors as well as orange, green, and purple, known as *secondary* colors (two primary colors mixed together). If you mix a primary color with a secondary color, you get an *intermediate* color such as yellow-green or red-orange. Intermediate color is sometimes called *tertiary* color.

COLOR

## Color Wheel

The *color wheel* illustrates how colors blend together. On the traditional color wheel shown here, you can see that the primary colors form a triangle. The three secondary colors form a second triangle. An intermediate color falls between each primary and secondary color.

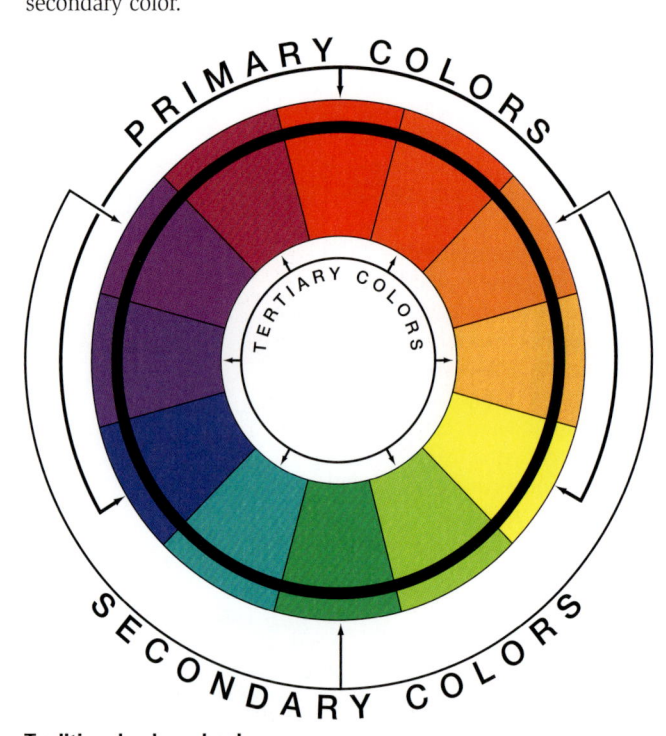

**Traditional color wheel**

When you are ready to paint, use the color wheel to choose a harmonious color scheme. This basic wheel has 12 colors—a combination of primary colors (red, yellow, blue), secondary colors (green, orange, purple), and six tertiary (or "mixed") colors.

The warm colors of the wheel include the reds, oranges, and yellows. The cool colors include the greens, blues, and purples. All the colors on the wheel are positioned in a specific place to help anyone create a pretty failsafe color scheme.

30   PAINTING

COLOR

When you are ready to create your own color scheme, play around with mixing complementary colors (those that are directly across from each other on the color wheel) and adding tertiary colors for a more interesting and pleasing effect. Once you get the hang of it, you will find mixing colors intriguing and fun.

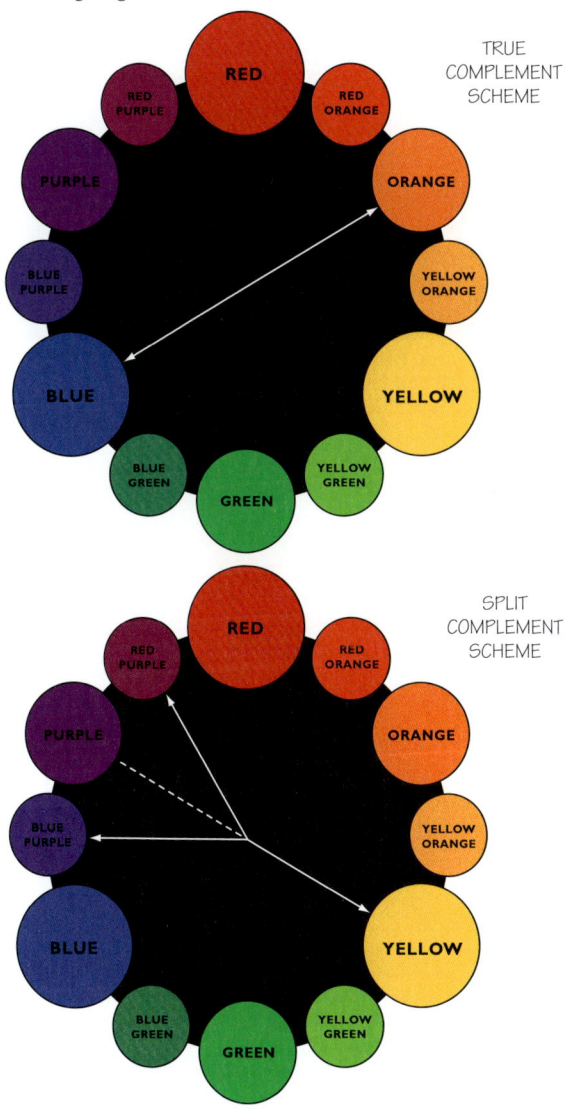

TRUE COMPLEMENT SCHEME

SPLIT COMPLEMENT SCHEME

Black, white, and gray are called neutral colors, which are neither "warm" nor "cold."

**PAINTING** 31

COLOR

During the Colonial era, the use of bold colors in a home was a sign of affluence. The pigments used to achieve these bright colors were costly, and only wealthy families could afford such a luxury.

**George Washington had the "small dining room" in his Mount Vernon residence painted a striking verdigris green. He believed the color to be "grateful to the eye" and less likely than other colors to fade.**

**The "south square room" of Thomas Jefferson's Monticello is painted a bright shade of blue that dates to the late 1800s. During Jefferson's time, however, this room, which served as the family sitting room, was unpainted plaster.**

Thomas Jefferson Foundation Inc./Robert C. Lautman, courtesy

32  PAINTING

COLOR

In contrast to the bolder colors of the Colonial era, these modern homes use muted colors for a more neutral background.

## Color Psychology

Color can alter the appearance of a room by making it appear smaller or larger, newer or brighter. It can also affect a person's mood. Research has shown that in a factory setting, a properly chosen color can make a more pleasant work environment, improve morale, increase production, and even help reduce accidents. Warm colors, such as red and yellow, can make a person feel physically warmer; cooler colors, like blue, make a person feel colder.

| Effect | Color | Usage |
|---|---|---|
| WARM | Yellow | Warm and welcoming, but also can heighten anxiety. Works well in narrow hallways and small entrance halls. Not for small bathrooms, as it gives your skin a yellowish cast—not too appealing when you look in the mirror! |
| | Orange | Cheerful and friendly; informal. Good in family rooms. |
| | Red | Stimulating; encourages action. Often used in restaurants. |
| COOL | Blue | Cool and calming. Used in bedrooms. |
| | Green | Relaxing and restful. Good for work and study environments. |
| | Violet | Power color, "royal" color. Found most often in places of worship. |
| NEUTRAL | Brown | Beiges coordinate easily with other colors. Good color in both work and living environments. |
| | Gray | Encourages creativity. Grays are more often used with other, brighter colors because when used alone it can impart a depressing tone (especially in northern climates). |
| | White | Reflects sophistication and cleanliness. Good around food and work environments such as the kitchen or sterile environments like hospitals. |
| | Black | Dignified, sleek, and sophisticated. It is usually used as an accent to enhance other colors. |

COLOR

Studies have revealed much about the influence color can have on one's mood, as well as good places to use certain colors.

## Effects of Light

Consider the amount of daylight a room receives when selecting a color. Using warmer, brighter, lighter colors in rooms with less sunlight may improve their appearance. Cooler, darker colors can balance the warmth of a well-lit room facing southwest.

Also, consider the function of the room and how light changes during the day. The bedroom with windows facing east may benefit from a warm color like yellow. This would stimulate a person in the morning wakeup hour and be inviting and cheerful later on and into the evening when the light is fading.

## Natural Light Versus Electric Light

Natural light, or sunlight, contains all colors. When a surface reflects sunlight and does not absorb any of its colors, it is called "white." When a surface absorbs all of its colors, it is called "black." An object that appears red will absorb all the colors of natural light except red. By contrast, electric light is artificial light that does not contain all colors. When it shines on an object, that object will reflect its own color and absorb all others. If the object's color is not present in the electric light, then the object cannot reflect it and will appear a different color.

PAINTING

## COLOR

There are two types of electric light—incandescent and fluorescent. Incandescent lighting is softer and has a yellow cast, whereas fluorescent lighting is much brighter and whiter. This is why the color a person likes so well in the local paint store often will look different on the wall at home. The best way to tell how a color will look is to review paint charts or chips (samples) in the room to be painted, and under different lighting conditions.

### Warm and Cool Lighting

Warm or cool lights affect people in the same way that warm or cool colors do. Use warm (incandescent) lighting to create a cozy effect. Use cooler lighting (fluorescent) to create a clean, bright, or orderly effect such as in a kitchen or office area.

### Balance Lighting and Color

Remember not to overdo it on one side or the other when matching color with lighting. If a very warm color is used with warm lighting, the result may be too "warm"—creating a sense of being cramped and stifled. Cooler whites used with fluorescent lighting, on the other hand, will create a very stark atmosphere that may seem cold and uninviting.

*Always balance warmth with coolness to create a pleasing effect.*

## Harmony

Combining colors also has special effect on a room. To make a small room seem larger, use one light color applied to walls, ceiling, and cabinets. To highlight a room, area, or cabinetry in a larger room, however, use a combination of light and dark colors.

Several color scheme types are available. *Analogous colors,* for example, are adjacent on the color wheel: green and yellow-green, for instance; or yellow-green and yellow.

*Complementary colors* are directly across from each other on the color wheel. These colors, together, form "completeness" of color, as they are always the sum of all three primary colors. Red and green (which is made of yellow and blue), for instance, are complementary colors. Use these colors in lighter or darker values for a pleasing, balanced effect.

PAINTING

COLOR

Imagine a line connecting complementary colors on the color wheel. If you split one end of that line in two as shown on page 31, you have a combination of three colors known as a *split complementary scheme.* Imagine those same three arrows, except pointing to colors equal distances from each other. Using a *triad scheme* can create some of the most beautiful color harmonies.

See the true complement and split complement schemes shown earlier in this chapter.

## How to Develop a Harmonious Color Scheme

1. Select a main color, which will be the dominant color.
2. Use lesser, unequal amounts of secondary or accent colors.
3. Create an overall color scheme for the entire house and integrate each room into it.
4. Match colors to the use of each room.
5. If you create a focal point with a dramatic *accent* color, carefully coordinate the other colors with it.
6. Remember that lighter colors tend to "open up" rooms visually, making them seem larger and brighter, and darker colors have the opposite effect.

## Color Matching

Most paint stores have sophisticated color-matching computer equipment for matching colors. Take a sample (paint chip or any solid, *opaque* material, such as a small piece of fabric, carpeting, upholstery, wallcovering, or even ceramic tile) of the desired color to the store.

The computer "reads" and "measures" the color components of the sample and compares it with formulas for colors. It then matches this with a "recipe" for *mixing* the paint.

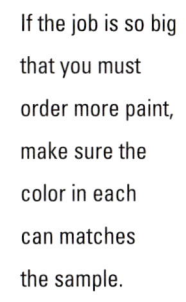

If the job is so big that you must order more paint, make sure the color in each can matches the sample.

**Paint chips and fabric swatches**

PAINTING 37

# All About Paint

Paint is made of four ingredients: pigment, resin, solvent, and additives.

- *Pigment* is finely ground color particles that, when mixed with a liquid, or *vehicle,* will provide—in addition to color—opacity, hardness, durability, and corrosion resistance.
- *Resin* is a natural or synthetic, transparent substance that attaches or "binds" to the pigment. Resins are also known as binders. Common *natural resins* come from trees and insects. Synthetic resins include alkyds, epoxies, silicones, vinyls, acrylics, polyurethanes, and polyesters. Most coatings are known by their resin type, such as alkyd, acrylic, epoxy, or coal tar epoxy.
- *Solvent,* often also known as *thinner,* is a liquid that dissolves paint for good spreading. Some classes of solvents include hydrocarbons, turpentines, ketones, esters, and glycol esters. Solvent also is used to clean painting equipment.
- *Additives* have many purposes. They help make the paint easier to apply. They enhance appearance. They improve durability and weathering. (See the introductory chapter for more information about the purposes for additives.)

## Oil-Based and Water-Based Paints

An *oil-based* paint contains *drying oil,* oil varnish, or oil-modified resin as the binder. Oil-based paints generally dry slower than water-based paints and have a strong odor. The final paint film—the *topcoat*—is formed by *oxidation,* the chemical process by which oxygen combines with the oil and hardens the paint. Most oil-based paints contain alkyds and epoxies, which allow the paint to dry harder and faster and to adhere better.

Since water-based paints contain no oil, they generally dry quickly and have less odor. The final paint film is formed through *evaporation* of the water. Water-based paints include latex and acrylic.

Both oil-based and water-based paints are used on indoor and outdoor surfaces.

## Ingredients and Functions of Solvent-Based Paints

**Alkyds** are synthetic resins used in paints and other protective coatings. Alkyd paint is oil-based, and its drying time depends on the type of oil used. Alkyds have a high durability for withstanding weathering and work well for exterior painting.

**Polyurethane** paints contain polyurethane resin. These durable paints *adhere* very well. Some polyurethanes are mixed with acrylic. These coatings are excellent for exterior use because of their durability, color retention, and resistance to *abrasion*.

## Ingredients and Functions of Water-Based Paints

**Latex** paint generally is made of water-based pigments, synthetic polymers like vinyl acrylics, and other chemicals. Latex paints are suitable for indoor and outdoor use, and cleanup is easy with soap and water.

**Acrylic** is a water-based paint popular for its excellent ability to retain color, for its durability and ease of application, and for its ease of cleanup with soap and water. Acrylics are appropriate for interior and exterior surfaces.

## Varnish

**Polyurethane varnish** is best used on everyday pieces that take a real beating. Drying time is fast. Polyurethane more closely resembles paint than wood.

**Oil-based varnish** is made with alkyd or phenolic resin. Phenolic varnishes yellow faster. Use oil varnish where resistance to weather is critical, such as on exterior floors, doors, and boat decks.

**Acrylic varnish,** a water-based varnish, does not penetrate wood as deeply as oil-based varnish. As a result, it is not as hard or as moisture-resistant, and it can appear dull and whitish when exposed to moisture. It may require more coats to achieve the same luster as solvent-based varnishes. While acrylic varnish can be more expensive than the oil-based type, it is more environmentally friendly. Cleanup is easier, too.

## Tinting

For your painting project, you probably purchased paint already mixed to the color you wanted. *Tinting* is the act of adding color to paint to produce a *shade* of that color. *Colorants* are pigments used to tint paint. Universal colorants can be used in oil-based or water-based paints. Tinted paint should have a uniform consistency and texture and produce a uniform color.

## The Importance of Sheen

*Sheen* is a critical characteristic that refers to the degree of shine or *gloss* of any coating or surface. The sheen currently on the surface can determine the amount of surface preparation required. Sheen affects the performance of the *finish coat:* the abrasion resistance, chemical resistance, and overall beauty of the painted area.

The typical full sheen range, from lowest to highest, includes *flat* or matte, *eggshell* or low luster, *satin* or pearl, *semigloss,* and high or *full gloss.* Because there are no industry-wide standard definitions of these terms, gloss levels may vary from one manufacturer to another.

The type of sheen you choose will depend on what you are painting. A flat finish is most often used for ceilings and on interior walls. It is not as "washable" as paints with more sheen. It works well for hiding imperfections on the surface being painted and for places where touch-ups may be necessary.

The eggshell finish has a slight sheen and is a popular choice for interior walls. Because it provides a good base for glazing and other special treatments, it is the ideal paint for decorative painting.

ALL ABOUT PAINT

Semigloss finish has a less porous surface and is perfect for trim, molding, doors, and windows. It is also used widely in kitchens and bathrooms—where easy cleanup is necessary—because this finish allows for easy cleanup. However, glossy finishes make touch-up marks and imperfections on the painted surface more visible.

**Flat finish**

> Besides environmental resistance, the other purpose of a finish coat is to provide a pleasing appearance—including the desired sheen. Since high-gloss coatings contain more resin, and more resistance to the effects of the elements, most exterior trim finish coats are made to have a gloss or semigloss appearance. Interior coatings use less resistant resins and, often, more pigment. These coatings can have a variety of sheens, from flat to glossy.

A coating's sheen is determined by its makeup. Full-gloss coatings with a smooth, highly reflective finish have a high ratio of resin to pigment. Less resin results in lower sheen. Flat finish coats contain much more pigment than resin.

**Glossy finish**

## Material Reducing

Always use the correct thinner, in the correct amount, mixed correctly with the paint. You can ruin paint by adding the wrong thinner or too much of it. Paint with too much thinner will not cover the surface.

Where thinning is concerned, never try to mix oil with water. Always refer to the product label if in doubt about the kind of thinner to use. With water-based paints, use plain tap water, and only in the amounts recommended on the label.

> Before thinning, mix the paint well. Paint that is too cold will thicken temporarily, so allow the paint to sit in a warm room to make it easier to spread. Cold paint may not need thinning, just warming.

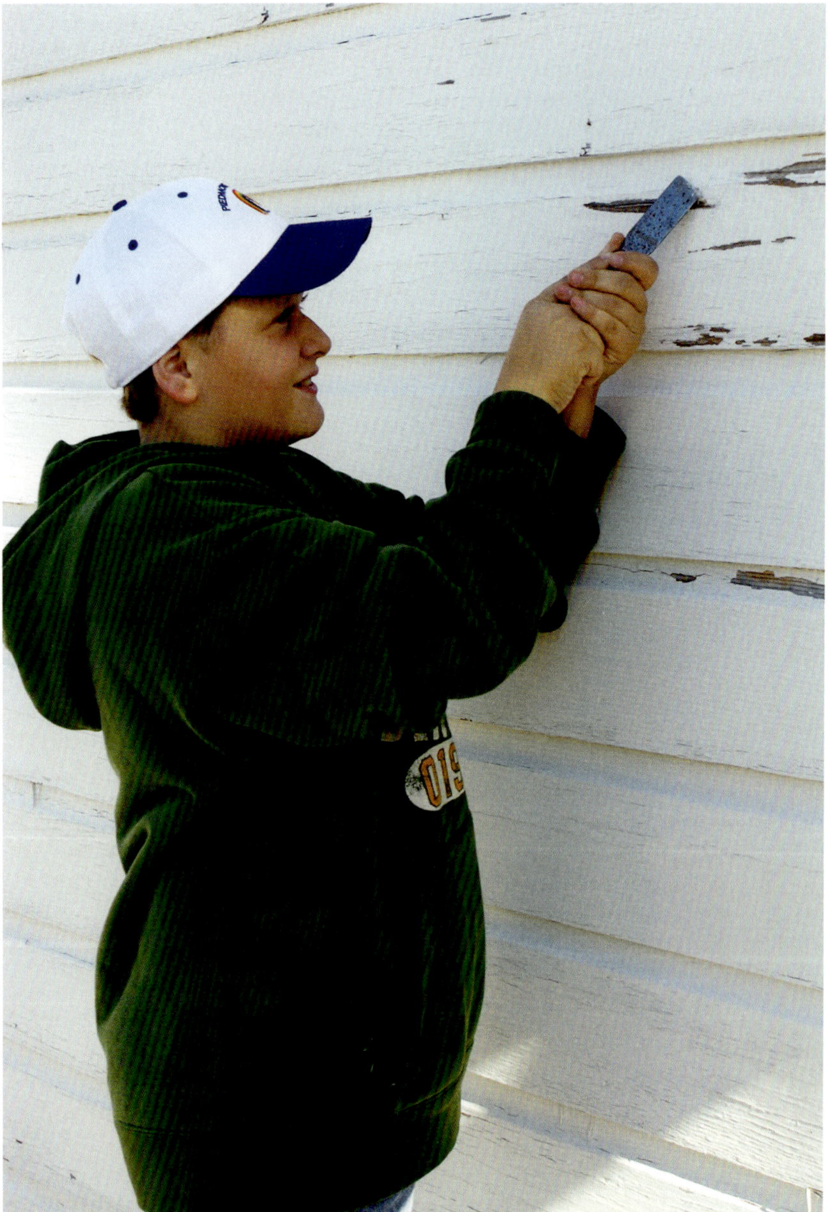

# Surface Preparation

*Surface preparation* is the most important—and often the most difficult and tedious—part of a painting job. The purpose is to create a clean, dry, sound surface to which paint can properly adhere. If this step isn't performed correctly, the paint will fail and your work will have to be redone. However, if the surface is prepared well, you will have the satisfaction of having painted something attractive that will last for years.

Consider the following factors when selecting a method of preparation:

- Type of surface and its condition
- Location and environment
- Coating to be used and manufacturer recommendations
- Any type of contamination on the surface
- Safety, health, and environmental regulations

## Cleaning the Surface

To begin, wash the area well with detergent to remove dirt, grime, oil, and grease. Use a household cleaner and an abrasive pad to remove any stubborn stains. Then rinse the surface with fresh water to remove residue. **Never** mix solvents or household cleaners. Doing so can produce hazardous gases.

> Remove *mildew* with a 3-to-1 solution of water and bleach or a commercial *fungicide;* let it dry thoroughly. Contact a local paint store for advice.

## Surface Preparation

### Wood

Before you paint, inspect the area to be painted and determine the condition of the wood. It should be dry, clean, sanded smooth, and dust-free. Remove all loose fibers, splinters, and rough spots by *sanding.* Always sand in the direction of the grain. New wood and bare wood should be primed to protect against weathering. This means to apply a coat of *primer,* which is a first coat that helps *adhesion* of additional coats.

For exterior wood in good condition, wash with soap and water to remove dirt, then rinse and let air dry. Washing with detergent effectively cleans very dirty exterior surfaces that are otherwise in good shape. Detergent must be thoroughly rinsed off and the surface allowed to thoroughly dry before proceeding.

Sand or scrape any areas of loose or cracked paint. Smooth the area until it blends with the surrounding area. Always remove all dust from the surface and surrounding area with a dry brush and *tack cloth* or (with interior jobs) a vacuum cleaner.

Scraping

Sanding

Scraped and sanded surface

## Concrete

Concrete can be cleaned with a broom, wire brush, vacuum, hand and power tools, and many other ways. Remove any oil or grease with a detergent or chemical cleaner; rinse thoroughly. After washing and rinsing, let the concrete dry completely before painting.

Fill holes with concrete or patching compound. Allow the patch to cure, or harden, properly. Use a wire brush to remove mortar spatter and other minor imperfections from new concrete surfaces.

Other methods that professionals use for treating concrete surfaces are abrasive blasting and acid etching, using a diluted acid to clean the surface.

## Metal

If the metal is rusting, use a wire brush or sandpaper to remove rust and particles. Wash metal surfaces (rusting or nonrusting) with an industrial-strength detergent. New factory-primed metal can be washed with an all-purpose detergent. Rinse thoroughly and dry with an absorbent cloth.

*Surface Preparation*

## Masking

*Masking* means protecting the areas surrounding your painting job using *painter's tape* and, if necessary, paper. Low-tack painter's tape is helpful around trim and doorways and works better than ordinary masking tape because it will not ruin the existing surface. For larger areas where protecting the existing surface is not a problem, it's OK to use masking tape. Apply the tape from the bottom up—work your way up from the floor—and then tape vertical areas. When the paint has dried, slowly peel away the tape at a 90-degree angle.

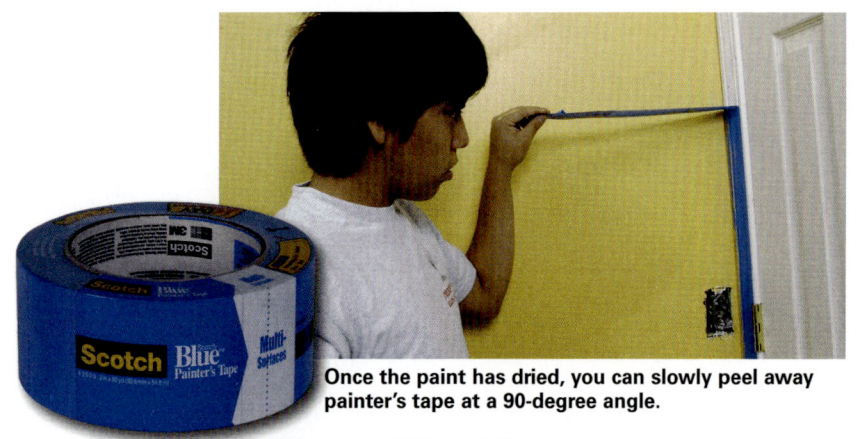

Once the paint has dried, you can slowly peel away painter's tape at a 90-degree angle.

## Patching and Repairing

**Step 1**—Before starting to paint you must fill any hairline cracks on porous surfaces. Dig out loose plaster with a putty knife or sharp scraper.

**Step 2**—Wipe the surface clean with a sponge.

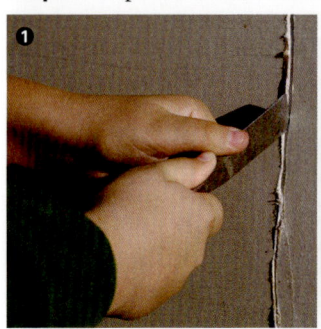

48   PAINTING

# Surface Preparation

**Step 3**—Fill the hole with *surfacing* or patching compound and let dry.

**Step 4**—Lightly sand the surface smooth and wash or wipe with a tack cloth to remove dust.

For cracks in concrete, use commercial *filler* made for concrete. After allowing it to dry, seal with a concrete sealer.

## Puttying

Fill nail holes, cracks, rough spots, and other imperfections in interior wood surfaces with putty. Handle the putty to soften it; if it is very hard, add a drop or two of linseed oil or mineral spirits. Apply with a putty knife or your finger and smooth it on so that it is even with the surrounding surface.

## Caulking

Use caulk to seal joints, fill cracks, and bridge gaps. Remove old caulk as well as dust and any loose material remaining. If the crack or joint being filled is more than $3/8$ inch wide, fill it first with backing material to get a good bond. The bead of caulk should be wide enough to fill the gap between the two surfaces, or gaps will form.

---

Store your putty in a sealed container. If you leave it out, it will harden and be wasted.

---

PAINTING

## Primer Selection

Applying primer, the first coat of paint, also is the last stage of surface preparation. The primer makes the next coat stick to the surface, protects the *substrate,* and seals the *surface.* There are different primers for wood, concrete and masonry, plaster and drywall, steel, and other metals.

**Primers for Wood.** Wood primers are available in oil-based or water-based products and can be used indoors or outdoors. Check the product label.

**Primers for Concrete and Masonry.** Exterior masonry surfaces are often highly alkaline, so be sure to use primers on surfaces that are alkali-resistant.

**Primers for Drywall and Plaster.** Make sure primers for plaster surfaces are alkali-resistant and that plaster dust is removed first. The best primers for drywall or gypsum board are water-based, such as vinyl and acrylic.

**Primers for Steel.** The type of primer you choose depends on the surface preparation required as well as the topcoat to be applied over the primer. Use an oil-based primer for poorly cleaned steel; synthetic primers require the steel to be thoroughly cleaned. Primers are available that penetrate well but cure to a hard, tough surface.

## Proper Use of Power Tools

Professionals use power tools when greater speed and effort are needed to clean a surface. These tools include grinders, sanders, power wire brushes, needle guns, and many others, including blasting tools and power washers. Professional painters know the importance of using these tools properly by following all safety guidelines and the manufacturer's instructions at all times.

Remember to follow these safety guidelines:
- Always wear goggles and gloves.
- Keep tools in good condition.
- Do not leave unused tools lying around.
- Never throw tools; use tools only for the purpose they were intended.
- Avoid using tools that make sparks near combustible liquids or vapors.
- Properly dispose of used rags throughout and at the end of each day.

SURFACE PREPARATION

## Proper Use of Hand Tools

Common hand tools include rags, sandpaper, abrasive pads, scrapers, broad knives and putty knives, wire brushes, and chipping hammers. Before using a scraper, brush, knife, or hammer, wash away oil and debris with detergents or solvents. Brush away or vacuum particles afterward.

1. Wire brushes clean debris from all types of surfaces.
2. The scraper removes paint from any type of surface.
3. A chipping hammer chips away layers of loose material from surfaces.
4. Use putty knives and broad knives to apply patching material and to scrape loose paint.
5. Use a cleaning brush to brush away debris and particles.

PAINTING

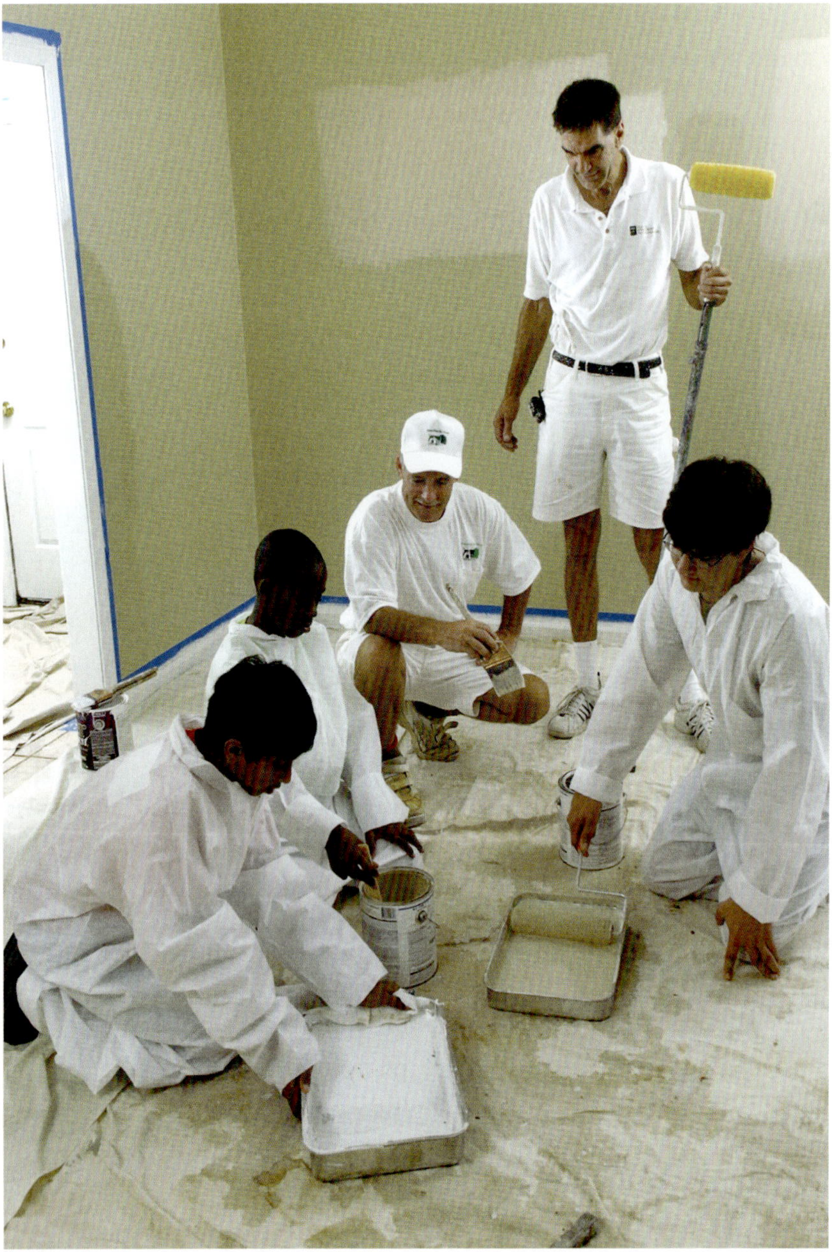

# Application Equipment and Procedures

A good paint job requires the right equipment and following the right procedures.

## Brushes

Use brushes for cutting in and painting areas that the roller can't reach. Try to use only quality brushes. Some brushes may be more expensive, but they may be worth it in the end because they will last longer and using them will give a better overall performance as you apply paint.

A *paintbrush* consists of four parts: the handle, the bristles, the epoxy setting that binds the bristles together, and the *ferrule*, which attaches the bristles to the handle.

Select a brush that is appropriate for the job and coating type. Use a synthetic brush when painting with latex paints. Make sure the brush holds the bristles tightly. Use natural bristles when using oil-based paints and varnish.

Choose brushes suitable in width for the specific job. For large areas, use a wall brush. Select a narrow sash brush for smaller, hard-to-get-to areas. For varnishing, use a thinner brush.

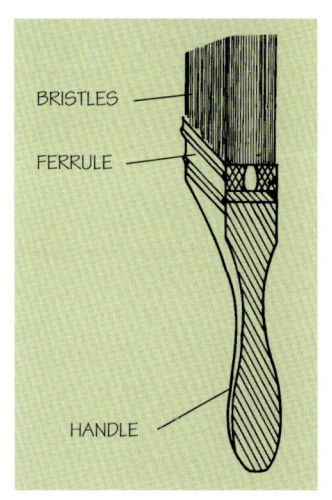

## Application Equipment and Procedures

Paint pads are rectangular foam pads covered with fabric and set in a plastic holder. These pads, with their straight sides, are useful for painting areas like the space between the ceiling and doorframe as well as exterior siding.

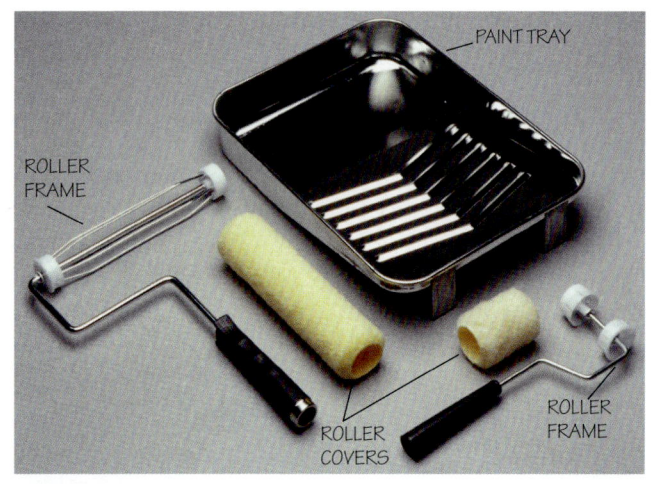

*Labels on image: PAINT TRAY, ROLLER FRAME, ROLLER COVERS, ROLLER FRAME*

### Rollers

Using rollers gets a paint job done quickly. There are two types of rollers: the more common dip roller, which is dipped into the paint for application; and the fountain or pressure roller, which has a hollow core where the paint is stored and pressure-fed through small pores to the outer fabric.

The fibers on the roller covers are known as the *nap,* usually described by the fiber length, which ranges from 1/4 inch to 1 3/4 inch. Generally, the rougher the surface you are painting, the longer the nap you should use. The longer nap makes it possible to work paint into irregular surfaces such as concrete block and highly textured walls like stucco. The smoother the surface you are painting—and the smoother the finish you want—the shorter the nap you should use.

Other equipment used with rollers includes extension poles, which can make it easier to reach higher places; trays; mesh grids, which are immersed in 5-gallon paint buckets to serve the same purpose as the rough edges in a roller tray; and special tools for cleaning roller covers.

= Application Equipment and Procedures

## Spray Systems

For professional painters, the most common spray-painting method is airless spraying. An airless sprayer uses a pump to pressurize the paint and force it through a tiny opening in the tip of the spray gun.

Air, or conventional, spraying uses compressed air to atomize paint into fine droplets as it leaves the spray gun. Conventional air spray offers the professional painter the greatest control for even application.

Spray paint also is available in aerosol cans.

**Professional painters always use the correct respirator when spraying or working near a spray system in use, and they make sure the area is well-ventilated.**

Drawbacks of spraying include overspray (which results in wastage), the need for considerable masking, and the additional protective equipment that this method requires. However, spray painting is the most productive application technique of all, especially over larger areas. It offers greater speed than other application methods.

PAINTING

Application Equipment and Procedures

## Care and Storage of Equipment

The most important part of taking care of any paint application tool or equipment is cleaning it immediately after painting. Failure to do so can cost you more time and more money spent on special cleaners, which in some cases may ruin the tool.

If you clean your brushes after each use, they will last a long time. Cleaning takes only a few minutes and saves hours of work and, quite possibly, the cost of replacement. If paint is allowed to harden in a brush, cleaning that brush becomes a difficult and time-consuming task—one that could have been easily avoided.

If the same brush and paint have been used over several days, store the brush for the night (with most of the paint wiped off) in tightly folded aluminum foil or wet paper.

Thoroughly clean brushes that have been used in oil paint with a solvent-based cleaner such as mineral spirits. (Follow the solvent cleaning by washing in warm sudsy water and rinsing.) If painting with water-based paint, clean the equipment well in soap and water, then rinse. Carefully smooth down the bristles and wrap the brush in its original packaging or heavy paper tied around the ferrule.

## Application Equipment and Procedures

Remove roller covers from the frame. Clean them thoroughly with the appropriate solvent or soap and water, and rinse well. Be sure to clean up around the painted area. After the paint has dried on the *drop cloth*, shake off any debris remaining on the cloth, then fold or roll it up neatly for storage. Sweep up the debris that you have shaken off and properly dispose of it.

## Coating Application Procedures

By this time, you should have chosen the type of paint to use for your project. You should also have studied your project and decided on an appropriate color or colors, and have properly prepared the surface for painting. You are now ready to paint.

### Getting Started

The painting process requires a few procedures to make the job go smoothly.

Be sure to calculate for additional coats and touch-ups. Unless they take up a major portion of the wall, there is no need to subtract for windows and doors.

PAINTING 57

## HOW MUCH PAINT?

Average house paint generally covers about 400 square feet per gallon, but this figure will vary. Read the label on the paint can before purchasing. Calculate the area you want to paint and compare that with the label to know how much paint to buy.

## Calculate This!

Here is how to determine the amount of paint needed for a rectangular or square area (say, a living room wall). Measure the height and the width, then multiply the two numbers.

**Example:**   8 feet height x 20 feet width = 160 square feet

To determine the area of a room you plan to paint, such as a living room, multiply the height and the width for each wall, then add the total for each wall.

**Example:**   8 feet height x 20 feet width = 160 square feet for wall 1

8 feet height x 20 feet width = 160 square feet for wall 2

8 feet height x 15 feet width = 120 square feet for wall 3

8 feet height x 15 feet width = 120 square feet for wall 4

160 + 160 + 120 + 120 = 560 square feet total

For the living room, you will need enough paint to cover 560 square feet. Depending on the type of paint you plan to use, you probably will need a little less than 2 gallons for the job.

### Material Preparation

Preparing paint for application includes mixing, thinning, tinting, and *straining*, when necessary. But first, be sure the work area is ready.

### Area Preparation

For interior areas, move furniture away from or out of the work area. Use drop cloths or newspaper to protect all remaining furniture, floors, and any other surface that should not be painted. Be careful about using newspaper as the ink may rub off on fabrics and carpet. Remove pictures and hardware before painting. Patch holes left by hangers if you won't be putting pictures back in the same place. Mask light switch plates, outlet covers, baseboards, and any trim work that needs to be protected.

## Application Equipment and Procedures

## Mixing

The ingredients in paint will separate and settle. To get adequate, even coverage, the paint must be mixed by any one (or a combination) of these methods:

- Stir with a wooden paint stick. (These sticks are usually available at your paint dealer at no cost.)
- Have the paint dealer shake it mechanically.
- *Box* the paint by stirring and then pouring it back and forth from one container to another to ensure a uniform color.

**Boxing**

## Thinning

New paint usually comes in the proper consistency and does not require thinning. If the paint has thickened, however, it may be necessary to add thinner.

Before thinning, mix your paint well and make sure it is at the proper temperature. Paint that is too cold may not need thinning, just warming. Because cold paint will be thicker than it should be, allow the paint to sit in a warm area so that it will have the proper consistency for spreading.

> Never use oil-based thinner with water-based paint, and never add water to oil-based paint. Using the wrong type of thinner, or using a thinner in the wrong amount, will ruin the paint. Refer to the paint can label to determine the right thinner to use, and the right amount to add. After thinning, always mix the paint well.

PAINTING

# Application Equipment and Procedures

**Straining**

**Straining**

If the paint has become lumpy, strain the paint through a wire screen, cheesecloth, or other straining device. Always make sure the paint is completely smooth, as lumps will harm the beauty and protective ability of the finished project. Oil-based paints tend to develop a "skin" on the surface from exposure to air. Do not mix this skin into the paint; lift it off, then strain the paint.

**Application Methods**

Common methods of applying paint are brushing, rolling, spraying, and using a pad. When deciding which method to use, consider the surface you are painting, its location and size, how fast the job needs to be done, and the type of paint.

Usually, a combination of the different methods is used. When painting a wall, for instance, use a brush to paint the areas next to the ceiling, trim work, and baseboards, then use a roller to quickly cover the larger area.

**Application Techniques**

> Master the trick of not having too much paint on the brush, and you will always have smooth, attractive surfaces.

It is best to pour a supply of paint into an empty, clean paint can (or another appropriate container) and work directly from this second container. Replenish your supply as needed. Begin painting the least accessible areas first. Grasp the brush firmly by the handle, holding it with the fingers on the ferrule just above the bristles. Keep the handle perpendicular to the surface. Dip the brush in the paint, just halfway up the bristles, and pat off the surplus on the inside (not the lip) of the can.

The basic brush technique for flat surfaces is to use short strokes in different directions to thoroughly cover an area about two square feet. Then even out the paint with a horizontal back-and-forth motion before reloading the brush. Start the next section about two feet below the first, working the paint into the previously painted area while the edges are still wet.

To minimize brush marks, *feather* the new paint. Lighten your touch as the layers overlap. Paint wood surfaces in the direction of the grain, and blend brush marks well on smooth surfaces.

60 PAINTING

## Application Equipment and Procedures

> Anything that is loose in the brush will end up on the wall. Before painting, make sure the brush is clean and in good repair. Loose bristles, dust, and dirt can leave specks on walls and give unsatisfactory results.

High-gloss *enamel* requires a different brush technique. Make three vertical brush strokes a brush-width apart. Without reloading your brush, make horizontal stripes across the three vertical ones, filling in the gaps and smoothing out the paint. Then, with the almost-dry paintbrush, go lightly over the section with vertical strokes. Reload the brush and repeat the process in the area below, blending it with the painted part.

**Allow plenty of time between coats for the paint to dry. See the label for drying times.**

For indoor painting, remember to keep the area well-ventilated with open windows or doors. Well-ventilated rooms dry more readily and are a safer and more comfortable work environment.

> If you notice the handle of the brush becoming wet with paint, stop and clean the brush with a clean, dry rag. Dip the brush halfway into the paint, but no more. Remember not to get too much paint in the brush.

**PAINTING** 61

Application Equipment and Procedures

## ROLLING

Rolling is a good technique for evenly covering a larger flat area or a rough surface such as brick, stucco, or concrete. First use a brush—which makes application in tight places easier to control—to paint any areas that are adjacent to places that should not be painted. For instance, when painting a wall in a house, use a brush to paint a strip along the edges of the wall near the ceiling and baseboard. Then, use the roller to cover the rest of the area more quickly, evenly, and effectively.

**Step 1**—Rub down the roller cover with your hand to remove loose nap. Make sure used rollers are clean and soft.

**Step 2**—Assemble the roller by sliding the roller cover over the cylinder on the roller frame.

**Step 3**—Fill the well of a paint tray about halfway with paint. Dip the roller into the paint and roll it across the ridged area of the tray to coat the roller. Plan to work in three-foot squares, which is about the coverage of one roller-load of paint.

**Step 4**—As you apply the paint, stroke the roller upward first to avoid splattering paint, then toward the strip painted with the brush. Roll back over the adjacent area to make the layer more even. Keep the pressure constant.

## APPLICATION EQUIPMENT AND PROCEDURES

## WOOD FINISHING

Wood finishing is the application of transparent or semitransparent coatings to protect the surface, accentuate the grain, and enhance the natural wood beauty.

**Interior Stains and Varnishes.** Interior *stains* are water-based and oil-based, and are specially designed for interior use. Unlike exterior varnishes, interior varnishes are not resistant to moisture or ultraviolet light. They are generally formulated to accentuate color, but they cannot make a surface opaque. However, interior varnishes do have certain characteristics to fit their functions. Floor varnish, for instance, has a high resistance to abrasion from heavy foot traffic.

## Applying Varnish

Applying varnish is similar to painting. Varnish is clear, making it more difficult to apply, so make sure lighting is adequate. The brush must be very clean. To avoid sags and runs, the brush should hold as much varnish as possible without dripping. Apply the varnish to a small area quickly, spreading it out evenly. Brush it first across the grain, then lightly with the grain to get a uniform thickness.

**Exterior Stains and Varnishes.** Exterior stains and finishing coats contain ingredients to protect the beauty of wood against the elements such as sun and rain. Stains come in a variety of colors and opacity, from nearly clear to opaque.

Basic wood-finishing projects generally need the following treatments, in order:

1. Using a putty knife, fill gouges and scratches in the wood surface with putty or wood dough.

2. Sand the wood smooth, if possible. Sand with the grain of the wood, using progressively finer grades of sandpaper. Make sure the surface is free of marks and dust, as any blemish left will show through on the finished project.

## Application Equipment and Procedures

3. Stain the wood surface to unify color and accentuate the wood grain. Colors range from clear, which highlights the grain, to dark, which hides the surface. Woods differ in their coloring capacity, depending on how porous they are. The same walnut stain that would produce a rich brown color on gumwood, for instance, could be nearly black on woods such as white pine, basswood, or poplar. Hardwoods, such as oak, maple, birch, walnut, and mahogany, often are left in their naturally beautiful state. Softwoods, such as pine, fir, and cypress, are suitable for staining to change their color or for a natural finish.

4. Seal the wood (particularly softwoods) with a *sealer* (or thinned varnish or *shellac*) to prime the stained wood. Follow the manufacturer's recommendation for the product.

5. Sand the surface again. Use a tack cloth to remove dust.

6. Varnish the wood (or use shellac or polyurethane). Apply finishing coats in the same way to each piece of wood (backs and fronts, sides, tops, bottoms) so all parts react evenly to moisture changes and won't warp. Some products combine procedures such as staining and sealing, or staining and finishing, for one-step applications.

### CONCRETE FINISHING

If the concrete surface is smooth (like a garage floor or porch), fill in any cracks before proceeding. With rough concrete block surfaces, block "fillers" often are used to help fill the porous surface. This substance can be rolled onto the surface using a long-napped roller to work the material into the pores of the block. Allow the block filler to dry completely before applying one or more finish coats.

> To paint a concrete floor, scrub it thoroughly with an abrasive detergent. Rinse it well and let it dry completely. Apply a coat of primer, followed by one or more coats of paint.

## METAL FINISHING

You can see metal finishes everywhere you look, from the ornamental decoration inside and outside homes to automobiles, commercial buildings, bridges, structures that support cities, and many other products.

Coatings for metal finishes are used to help prevent corrosion, provide resistance to abrasion and wear, add color, improve appearance, and make cleanup and maintenance easier. Spray painting is the most popular method for painting metal.

Remove any old flaking paint and rust with a wire brush or sandpaper. Sand any glossy surfaces to help ensure good adhesion for subsequent coats of paint. Check that all bolts or railings are secure. Dust off the metal surface and wash down with a metal preparation solution, solvent, or detergent.

Apply one coat of anti-rust primer over the entire area and allow to dry according to instructions on the label. Then apply one or two coats of finish paint. Follow the paint can label for drying instructions.

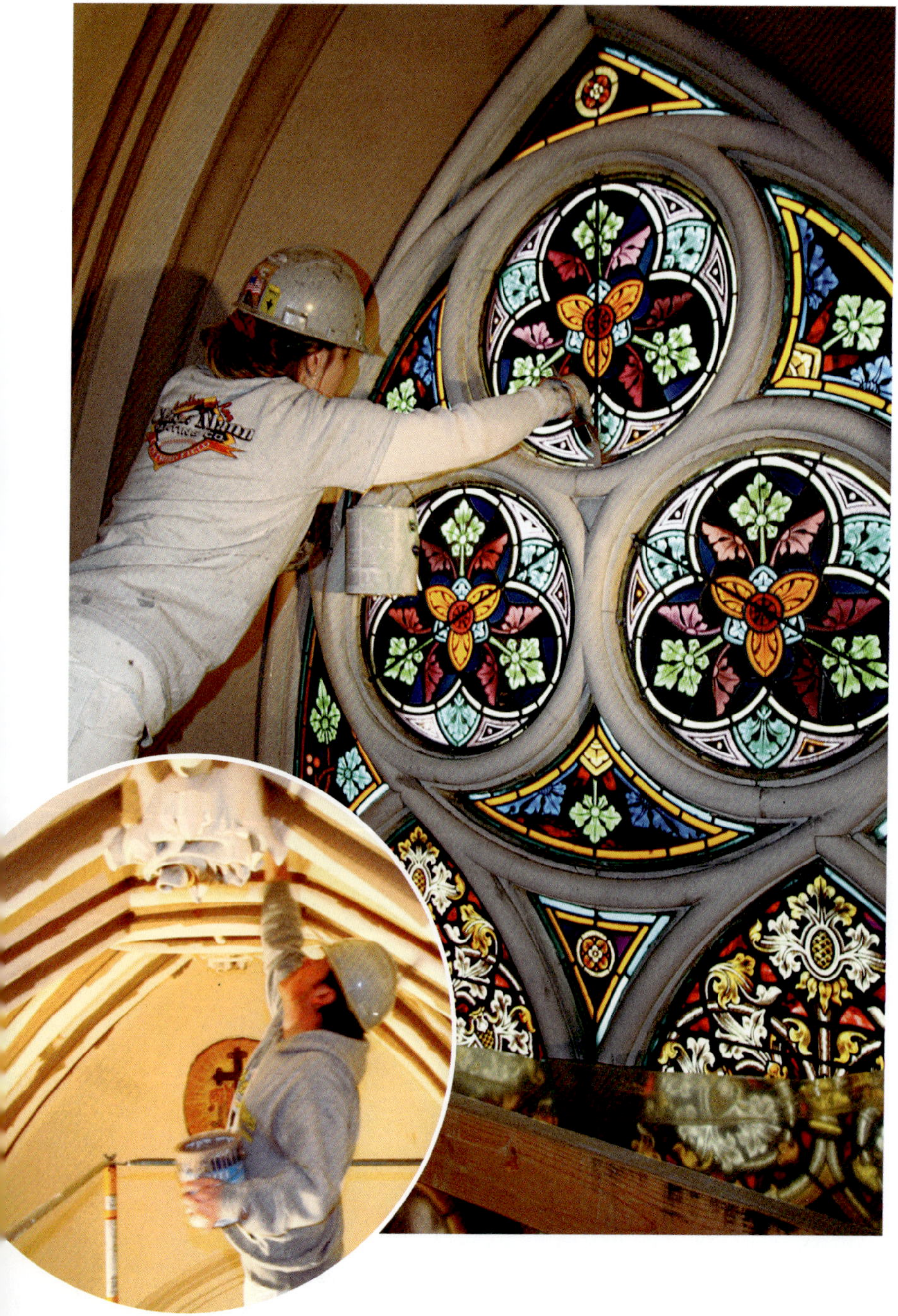

# Opportunities in the Painting Craft

Many options are available to someone interested in training in the painting craft.

If you have a knack for and enjoy the skills and activities involved in painting, you would likely enjoy the profession itself. Painting is demanding work and requires good eyesight and health, as well as physical strength and dexterity. The professional must demonstrate some degree of the artistic appreciation and ability necessary to define color schemes and mix colors. Lastly, you must be intelligent, friendly, and have a knack for pleasing your customer.

In some areas of the country, painting does have a seasonal nature, which means you must save money when you are working for the times when you may not be. Physical injury is always a risk when you spend a good deal of time climbing ladders and scaffolding or handling chemicals. However, these risks are minimized when you prepare and plan ahead.

> The advantages of painting as a career include its relative ease to learn, good pay, and personal satisfaction in the improvements you make on your customers' environment. You often work outdoors and often are your own boss. You will rarely work in the same location or do the same job for long.

## Training in the Craft

The best way to learn the painting craft is to get on-the-job training. A three-year *apprenticeship* is a satisfactory way to get not only the training but also the experience necessary to secure your own position right away.

> The Painting and Decorating Contractors of America is the nation's largest trade association serving the educational needs of the painting and decorating craftsperson and contractor. Membership is voluntary, and benefits range from business training, to safety, to participation in the development of industry standards and publications, and most importantly the exposure to a network of contractors who freely interact with each other to improve the painting and wallcovering industry. See the resources section for more information.

*Check community colleges in your area to find trade courses in the construction and painting industries.*

Sadly, fewer than 10 percent of all painting and decorating contractors participate in a professional trade association. As businesses become more complex with new regulations, the need for continuing education becomes more important.

Many chapters of professional trade organizations throughout the country, like the Painting and Decorating Contractors of America, have apprenticeship-training programs in place. The International Union of Painters and Allied Trades offers three-year apprenticeship programs and training in the removal of lead-based paint.

Another source of information is the National Center for Construction Education and Research, which offers information on how to find training in the painting craft that may be available in your area.

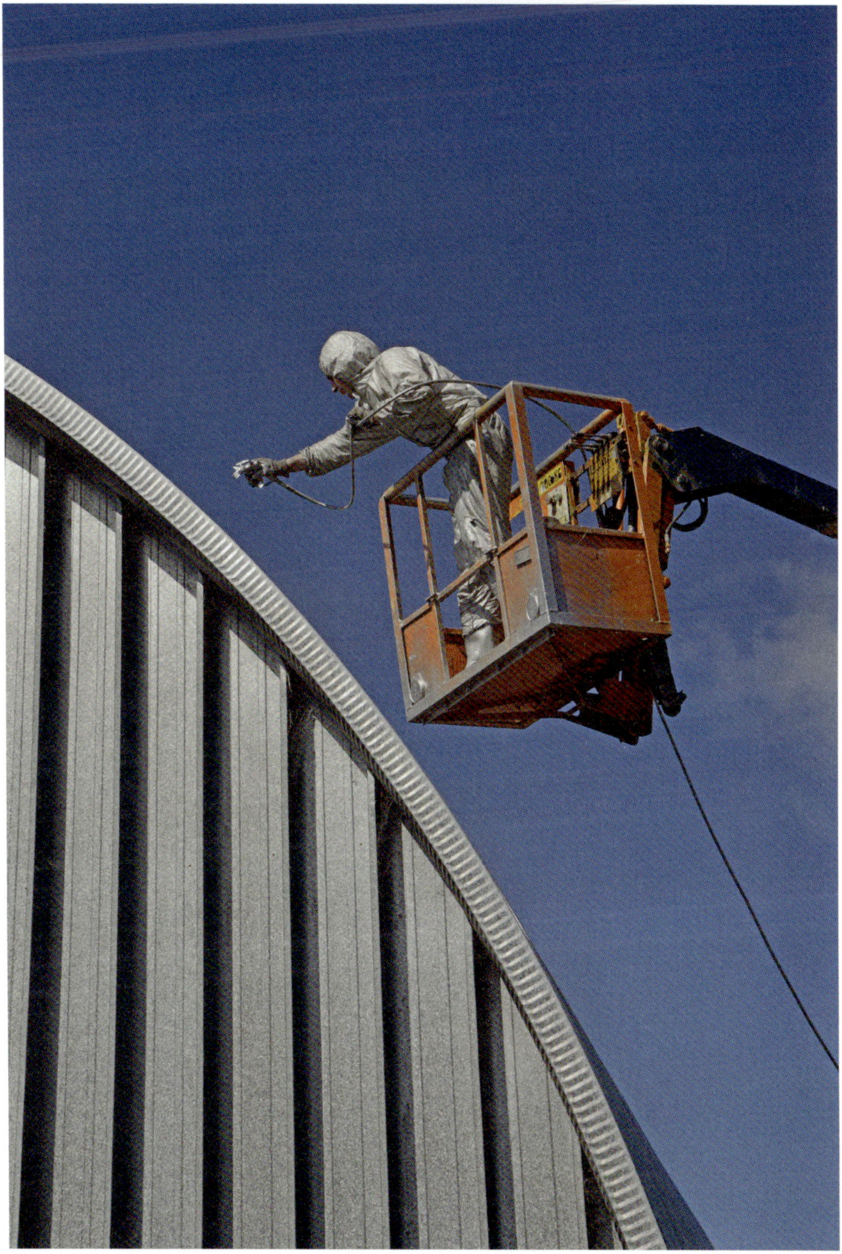

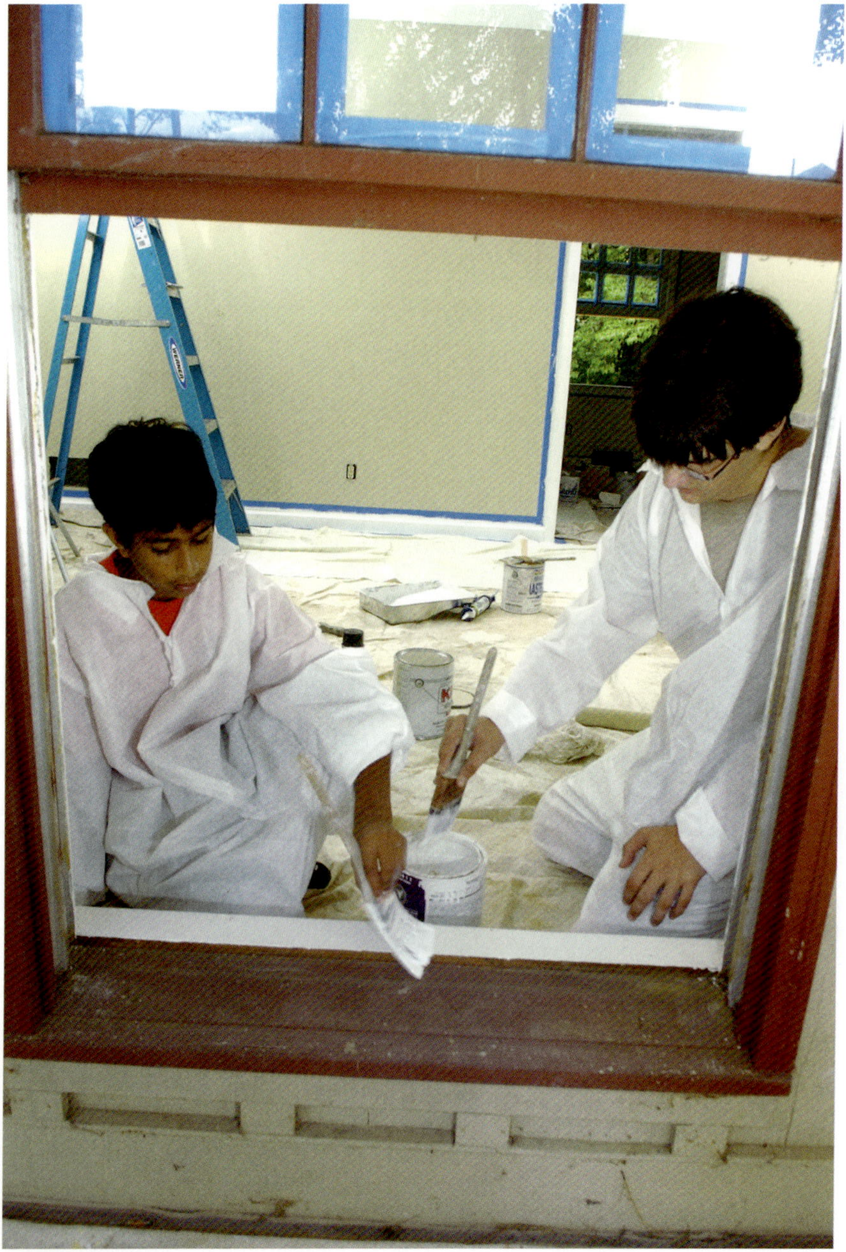

# Glossary

**abrasion.** The wearing down or removal of a surface with an abrasive material.

**accent.** In decorating, a bright object or color that draws attention.

**acrylic paint.** A synthetic resin- and water-based paint popular for its ability to retain color, its durability, and its ease of application and cleanup.

**additive.** A substance added to a coating to adjust, enhance, or improve it.

**adhesion.** The degree of attraction between a coating and a substrate or between two coatings.

**alkyd.** A type of synthetic resin used in coatings. An alkyd paint is oil-based. *See also* resin.

**analogous colors.** Colors that are beside each other on the color wheel.

**apprenticeship.** On-the-job training under the guidance of a skilled craftsperson.

**binder.** The paint ingredient that binds pigment particles together and makes them adhere to a surface. Resins and oils are examples of binders.

**boxing.** Mixing paint by pouring it from one container to another several times. *See also* mixing.

**brush.** *See* paintbrush.

**colorant.** Any substance that adds color to another material or mixture. *See also* shade *and* tint.

**color pigment.** Organic or inorganic substance that provides color to a paint.

**color spectrum.** The distribution of colors produced when sunlight is dispersed by a prism.

**color wheel.** A round diagram of the color spectrum, showing the relationships between colors.

**complementary colors.** Two colors that are opposite each other on the color wheel.

# Glossary

**drop cloth.** A large piece of canvas or plastic used to protect the surrounding area and furniture from damage.

**drying oil.** An oil that serves as a binder in oil-based paint and converts to a solid film when exposed to oxygen.

**eggshell.** A level of gloss between semigloss and flat.

**enamel.** Topcoat that is characterized by its ability to form a durable high-gloss surface.

**evaporation.** The process in which the paint binder solvent (water) converts to a vapor, leaving a dried combination of pigment and resin on the surface.

**faux finishes.** Decorative application of solid color coats and glazes to simulate marble, granite, wood grain, and so on.

**feather.** To taper off the edge of a layer of paint.

**ferrule.** The metal band that binds the bristles to the paintbrush handle.

**filler.** A substance used to fill cracks, pores, etc., in a surface before painting or varnishing. *See also* wood filler.

**finish coat.** The last layer of coating in a painting operation. *See also* topcoat.

**flammable.** Capable of igniting easily and burning quickly.

**flat.** A coating that lacks luster or gloss in the dried form.

**full gloss.** An almost mirrorlike surface when viewed from all angles.

**fungicide.** An additive that helps resist the growth of fungus (mildew).

**gloss.** The relative amount and nature of a surface's reflection.

**inorganic.** A compound that does not share the characteristics of living things (plants and animals) and generally is derived from minerals.

**intermediate color.** The result of mixing a primary and secondary color.

**lacquer.** A liquid consisting of organic or synthetic resins dissolved in a quick-drying solvent. When the solvent evaporates, the resins adhere to the coated surface, producing a hard, smooth high-gloss finish.

**latex paint.** A water-based paint having a synthetic rubber or plastic binder.

**lead-based paint.** Any coating that contains lead in excess of limits established by the U.S. government. Because of its dangers, lead in household paint has been banned by the Consumer Product Safety Commission since 1978. Lead paint should be removed only by a professional.

# Glossary

**masking.** The procedure of covering surfaces adjacent to the painting area with a low-tack adhesive (painter's) tape; paper also is sometimes used.

**mildew.** A fungus that grows on paint and other materials in damp places, causing discoloration and deterioration. *See also* fungicide.

**mineral spirits.** A solvent used for thinning oil-based paint. *See also* solvent.

**mixing.** Combining all ingredients in a paint to create a uniform liquid with even color and texture. *See also* boxing.

**nap.** The fibers on a paint roller cover, generally described in terms of length.

**natural resin.** A resin originating in certain plants or insects. *See also* resin.

**oil-based coating.** A paint that contains drying oil, oil varnish, or oil-modified resin as the basic vehicle ingredient.

**oil stain.** A solution of dye in a blend of oil or varnish and aromatic solvent.

**opaque.** Blocking rays of light; not transparent.

**organic.** Generally, a compound containing carbon and having originated from a plant or animal.

**oxidation.** The process in which the paint binder solvent (oil) chemically combines with oxygen and hardens the paint.

**paintbrush.** A tool made of natural or synthetic bristles set into a handle.

**painter's tape.** A special tape much like masking tape used in the masking process to help protect areas adjacent to the area being painted. This low-tack tape is easy to remove and will not damage existing painted areas.

**paint failure.** The premature deterioration of a coating resulting from problems of workmanship, substrate conditions, material, coating, exposure, or a combination of these factors.

**painting.** The craft of improving the surface of a structure, furniture, etc., by applying coatings to that surface. The craft includes many processes, such as selecting appropriate materials and preparing surfaces to accept the coatings.

**paint roller.** A paint application tool with a fabric-covered tube that fits over a handled frame, designed to roll paint onto a surface.

**paint tray.** A tray with a well for holding paint and a rough-textured ramp for working paint into a roller cover.

**pigment.** *See* color pigment.

# Glossary

**power washing.** The use of pressurized water with or without detergents or additives to clean a surface of contaminants and debris.

**primary colors.** The three pigments of red, yellow, and blue, which cannot be produced by any mixture of other pigments.

**primer.** The first coat in a painting operation, designed to promote adhesion of subsequent coats.

**resin.** A natural or synthetic, transparent substance that attaches or "binds" to the pigment in a coating.

**respirator.** A mask covering the nose and mouth to either supply breathable air or filter impurities from the air.

**safety data sheet.** A sheet of product information required by the U.S. government identifying hazardous chemicals, health and physical hazards, exposure limits, and precautions for employees in the workplace.

**sanding.** The act of leveling and smoothing a surface before paint or stain is applied. The surface is rubbed with an abrasive paper or sanding machines.

**satin finish.** A dried paint film with a luster resembling satin. Ranks between eggshell and semigloss.

**sealer.** A coat of thinned varnish or shellac to prime wood before staining, or after staining to penetrate the wood and limit the number of finish coats required.

**secondary color.** The color produced by mixing equal amounts of two primary colors. The secondary colors are orange, green, and purple. *See also* primary colors.

**semigloss.** A gloss range between full gloss and eggshell.

**shade.** A color to which black has been added. The opposite of tint.

**sheen.** The degree of luster of a dried, fully cured paint film.

**shellac.** A lacquer made from a natural resin deposited on twigs by the lac insect of Asia.

**solvent.** A liquid that dissolves paint further for good spreading. Also known as thinner.

**split complementary scheme.** The combination of a base color with two colors flanking its complement on the color wheel.

**stain.** A transparent or semitransparent coating that colors a substrate, usually wood, without hiding the grain or other texture.

**stenciling.** Applying a design to a surface by brushing ink or paint through a cutout pattern.

# Glossary

**straining.** The removal of large particles from mixed paint by pouring it through a wire screen, cheesecloth, or other straining device.

**substrate.** Any surface to which paint, coating, or wallcovering is applied.

**surface.** The substrate to which paints are applied.

**surface preparation.** Treatment of a surface, such as washing, filling, puttying, cleaning, or power cleaning, to prepare it for coating.

**surfacing compound.** A quick-drying surface compound used to patch plasterwork, fill cracks and holes, and provide a smooth surface for painting.

**tack cloth.** A clean, lint-free cloth treated with diluted varnish to make it sticky, for removing dust from a surface.

**tertiary color.** The result of mixing two secondary colors.

**thinner.** See solvent.

**tint.** A color to which white has been added. The opposite of shade.

**tinting.** Adjusting the color of paint to a wide range of tints, shades, or tones.

**tone.** The result of adding both black and white to a color. See also *shade* and *tint*.

**topcoat.** The finish coat of a coating system, designed to add beauty or protection. See also *finish coat*.

**toxin.** A poisonous substance.

**triad scheme.** The combination of any three colors equidistant on the color wheel.

**undercoat.** Any coat applied after the primer and prior to the finish coat.

**varnish.** A liquid containing resins and/or oils that dries to a translucent or transparent solid film after application.

**vehicle.** Composed of binder and solvent, the liquid portion of paint in which the pigment is dispersed.

**vinyl resin.** A synthetic resin made from vinyl compounds. See also *resin*.

**wood filler.** A substance made of crushed quartz and pigments mixed with a binder and driers. It is used to fill the pores in wood to produce a very smooth finish or to enhance the grain pattern of the wood.

PAINTING

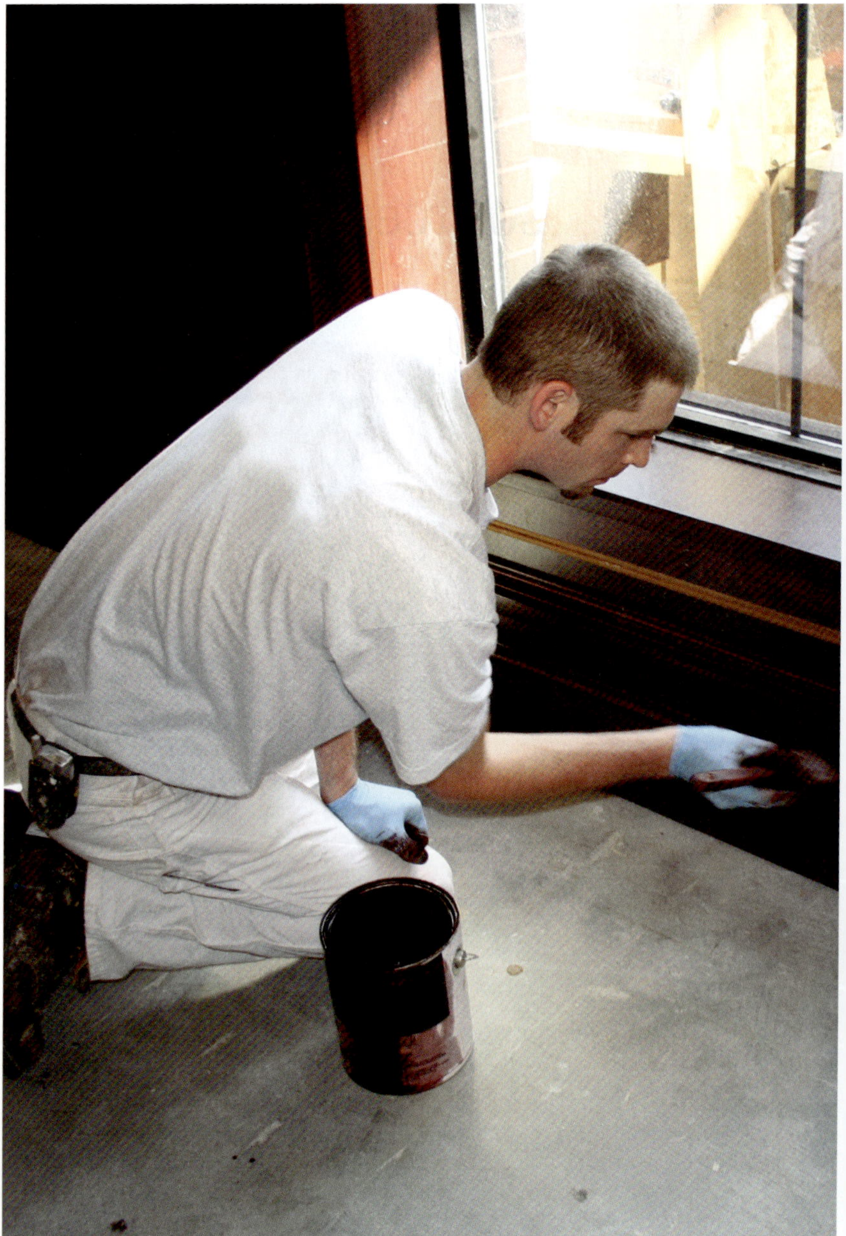

# Painting Resources

## Scouting Literature
*Home Repairs* and *Safety* merit badge pamphlets

> With your parent's permission, visit the Boy Scouts of America's official retail website, www.scoutshop.org, for a complete listing of all merit badge pamphlets and other helpful Scouting materials and supplies.

## Books

Becker, Holly, and Joanna Copestick. *Decorate: 1,000 Professional Design Ideas for Every Room in Your Home.* Chronicle Books, 2011.

Better Homes and Gardens. *Decorative Paint Techniques and Ideas,* 2nd ed. Better Homes and Gardens, 2009.

Donegan, Francis. *Paint Your Home: Skills, Techniques, and Tricks of the Trade for Professional Looking Interior Painting.* Reader's Digest Association Inc., 1997.

Eiseman, Leatrice. *Colors for Your Every Mood: Discover Your True Decorating Colors.* Capital Books, 2000.

*Essential Paint Techniques: Improving Your Home With Paint Inside and Out.* This Old House Books, 2000.

McElroy, William. *Painter's Handbook.* Craftsman Book Company, 1988.

*Painting and Decorating Craftsman's Manual and Textbook.* Painting and Decorating Contractors of America, 1995.

Sloan, Annie. *Quick and Easy Paint Transformations: 50 Step-by-Step Ways to Makeover Your Home for Next to Nothing.* CICO Books, 2015.

Starmer, Anna. *The Color Scheme Bible: Inspirational Palettes for Designing Home Interiors.* Firefly Books, 2012.

Travis, Debbie, and Barbara Dingle. *Debbie Travis' Decorating Solutions: More Than 65 Paint and Plaster Finishes for Every Room in Your Home.* Clarkson Potter, 1999.

Wilbur, C. Keith. *Homebuilding and Woodworking in Colonial America.* Chelsea House Publishers, 1997.

## Painting Resources

## Organizations and Websites

### American Coatings Association
Website: http://www.paint.org
The ACA is a nonprofit organization "working to advance the needs of the paint and coatings industry and the professionals who work in it." Its website provides information about proper paint disposal, as well as technical and educational materials.

### BEHR
Website: http://www.behr.com
This paint company's internet site provides helpful links that offer such things as how-to questions and answers and a calculator that estimates the amount of paint needed for a particular project.

### Better Homes and Gardens
Website: http://www.bhg.com/decorating/paint/decorative-painting/
This site provides tips and techniques for creating decorative wall patterns and murals.

### Environmental Protection Agency
Website: http://www.epa.gov/lead/pubs/renovation.htm
This site explains the EPA's Renovation, Repair, and Painting rule that applies to companies working on certain projects that disturb lead-based paint.

### Handyman Wire
Website: http://www.handymanwire.com
This site offers "expert advice and help for do-it-yourselfers" and allows users to post questions to experts.

### International Union of Painters and Allied Trades
Website: http://www.iupat.org
The IUPAT is a labor union that helps ensure safe working conditions and good wages and benefits for its more than 160,000 members. The website provides an extensive history of the union, union news and events, information on training and education in the trades, updates on current political and community affairs, and links to district and regional offices across the country.

### Kelly-Moore Paints
Website: http://www.kellymoore.com

### National Center for Construction Education and Research
Website: http://www.nccer.org
The NCCER develops and publishes standardized construction and maintenance curricula, safety programs, management education, industry image materials, and craft skill assessments.

### National Lead Information Center
U.S. Environmental Protection Agency
Website: http://www.epa.gov/lead/forms/lead-hotline-national-lead-information-center
This arm of the Environmental Protection Agency provides painting professionals and the general public with information about lead hazards and their prevention.

### The Old House Web
Website: http://www.oldhouseweb.com
This site gives "old-house enthusiasts" ideas and advice on many home improvement tasks, products, and suppliers.

# Painting Resources

### The Paint Quality Institute
Website: http://www.paintquality.com
The Paint Quality Institute was founded to educate "consumers, contractors, and retailers on the advantages of using the highest quality paints and coatings." The website contains a wealth of information on safety, paint ingredients, and decorative techniques.

### Painting and Decorating Contractors of America
Website: http://www.pdca.org
The official website of the Painting and Decorating Contractors of America is a resource for the professional painting contractor and the home do-it-yourselfer as well.

### This Old House
Website: http://www.thisoldhouse.com

## Acknowledgments

Thanks to Barbara Richardson and Jerry Glica of Glidden Professional (formerly known as ICI Dulux Paints), Cleveland, Ohio, for their assistance with the traditional color wheel found in this pamphlet.

Thanks to The Sherwin-Williams Company for use of its safety data sheet on page 25.

The Boy Scouts of America is grateful to the men and women serving on the National Merit Badge Subcommittee for the improvements made in updating this pamphlet.

---

The Boy Scouts of America is grateful to Charles "Chuck" Mann IV, Chas. F. Mann Painting Company, Toledo, Ohio, for his assistance with revising the *Painting* merit badge pamphlet. This dedicated Scouter is a former president of the Painting and Decorating Contractors of America. The BSA also is thankful to PDCA members Paul Corey, Mike Sanford, Mike Ausherman, and Ken Anderson.

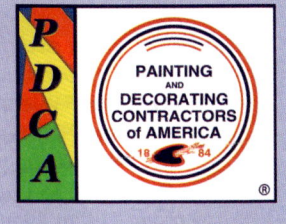

PAINTING  79

## Photo and Illustration Credits

Charles F. Mann IV, courtesy—pages 66 *(stained glass windows, painter)*, 67, and 68

Mount Vernon Ladies' Association, courtesy—page 32 *(Mount Vernon)*

Jerry Padier, courtesy—page 10

The Sherwin-Williams Company, courtesy—page 25

Shutterstock.com—cover (*roller tray,* ©Dmitrij Skorobogatov; *swatches,* ©tobkatrina; *paint bucket,* ©Len Green; *masking tape,* ©autsawin uttisin) and pages 2 (©varuna), 3 (©Len Green), 4 (©GoodMood Photo), 5 (©tobkatrina), 6 (©pedrosala), 8 (*house,* ©Gerald A. DeBoer; *barn,* ©Paula Cobleigh), 13 (©Kokhanchikov), 15 (©pryzmat), 17 (©Kordik), 22 (*paint cans,* ©IkeHayden), 23 (©Rob Bayer), 27 (*cracked paint,* ©pzAxe).
©aliced
Samok
Razum
33 (*ki*
©Mark
*dinin*
36 (*la*
©Cha
37 (©
41 (©
*purpl*
©Zep

Hontovyy), 47 (*concrete floor,* ©Andy Dean Photography; *scrollwork,* ©audioscience), 54 (*painter,* ©bikeriderlondon), 55 (*spray paint can,* ©Ollyy; *painter,* ©Lakeview Images; *spray gun,* ©KKulikov), 56 (©-Taurus-), 58 (©Peter Wollinga), 63 (©rjmiguel), 65 (©Elena Elisseeva), 69 (©Lakeview Images), 71 (©Kameel4u), 72 (©Sheri Herbert), and 73 (*roller tray,* ©Dmitrij Skorobogatov)

Thomas Jefferson Foundation Inc./ Robert C. Lautman, courtesy—page 32 (*Monticello*)

Wikipedia.org, courtesy—pages 11 and 21

All other photos and illustrations are the property of or are protected by the Boy Scouts of America.

Dan Bryant—pages 14, 16, and 51

Daniel Giles—pages 12, 52, and 70

...illustrations on
6, 28
*roller,*
6 *(scraping,*
*ed surface),*
*2),* 49
, 59,
*se-up),*
*p 4),*